Ali-Cina Fahimi

The truth behind Germany's intervention in Afghanistan

A case study on the ground

Anchor Compact

Fahimi, Ali-Cina: The truth behind Germany's intervention in Afghanistan: A case study on the ground. Hamburg, Anchor Academic Publishing 2014
Original title of the thesis: A terrorism threat for Germany or serving political-economic interests? A case study of Germany's intervention in Afghanistan

Buch-ISBN: 978-3-95489-287-7
PDF-eBook-ISBN: 978-3-95489-787-2
Druck/Herstellung: Anchor Academic Publishing, Hamburg, 2014

Bibliografische Information der Deutschen Nationalbibliothek:
Die Deutsche Nationalbibliothek verzeichnet diese Publikation in der Deutschen Nationalbibliografie; detaillierte bibliografische Daten sind im Internet über http://dnb.d-nb.de abrufbar

Bibliographical Information of the German National Library:
The German National Library lists this publication in the German National Bibliography. Detailed bibliographic data can be found at: http://dnb.d-nb.de

All rights reserved. This publication may not be reproduced, stored in a retrieval system or transmitted, in any form or by any means, electronic, mechanical, photocopying, recording or otherwise, without the prior permission of the publishers.

Das Werk einschließlich aller seiner Teile ist urheberrechtlich geschützt. Jede Verwertung außerhalb der Grenzen des Urheberrechtsgesetzes ist ohne Zustimmung des Verlages unzulässig und strafbar. Dies gilt insbesondere für Vervielfältigungen, Übersetzungen, Mikroverfilmungen und die Einspeicherung und Bearbeitung in elektronischen Systemen.

Die Wiedergabe von Gebrauchsnamen, Handelsnamen, Warenbezeichnungen usw. in diesem Werk berechtigt auch ohne besondere Kennzeichnung nicht zu der Annahme, dass solche Namen im Sinne der Warenzeichen- und Markenschutz-Gesetzgebung als frei zu betrachten wären und daher von jedermann benutzt werden dürften.

Die Informationen in diesem Werk wurden mit Sorgfalt erarbeitet. Dennoch können Fehler nicht vollständig ausgeschlossen werden und die Diplomica Verlag GmbH, die Autoren oder Übersetzer übernehmen keine juristische Verantwortung oder irgendeine Haftung für evtl. verbliebene fehlerhafte Angaben und deren Folgen.

Alle Rechte vorbehalten

© Anchor Academic Publishing, ein Imprint der Diplomica® Verlag GmbH
http://www.diplom.de, Hamburg 2014
Printed in Germany

Table of Contents

Abbreviation Index 2
Acknowledgments 3
Abstract 5
Introduction 7
   A) Background 7
   B) Structure & Research question 8
   C) Methodology & case study 10
   D) Literature Review 12
   E) Theoretical Framework 17

1. Analysis of Germany's official story - a security threat from Afghanistan 19

2. Examination of Germany's hypothesis 23
   2.1. International Terrorism 23
   2.2. AQ & Taliban 24
   2.3. Analysis of available terrorism data 25
   2.4. Reassessment of the German story 28

3. Analysis of the reasons for the German approach 32
   3.1. Afghanistan – an opportunity to implement an elitist consent 32
   3.2. Hegemony and world order – A Gramscian perspective 36

4. Analysis of further political-economic interests 41
   4.1. A cost-benefit analysis 41
   4.2. Geopolitical benefits 45

Conclusion 47
Bibliography 50

Abbreviation Index

AQ	Al-Qaeda
ANA	Afghan National Army
ANSF	Afghan National Security Forces
ANP	Afghan National Police
ASEAN	Association of South East Asian Nations
DGAP	Deutsche Gesellschaft für Auswärtige Politik (German Council on Foreign Relations)
DIW	Deutsches Institut für Wirtschaftsforschung (German Institute for Economic Research)
IMF	International Monetary Fund
IO	International Organisation
ISAF	International Security Assistance Force
KSK	Kommando Spezialkräfte (Special Forces Command)
NGO	Non-governmental Organization
NATO	North Atlantic Treaty Organization
SWP	Stiftung Wissenschaft und Politik (German Institute for International and Security Affairs)
UN	United Nations

Acknowledgments

First of all, I would like to thank my parents, without whom my first journey to Afghanistan during this difficult security environment would not have been possible. I also would like to express my deepest appreciation to the hospitality of the Afghans and the enlightening interviews of the participants during my research trip in Afghanistan. Finally, I would like to thank Yasmin Granfar. She is an amazing and wonderful person, who inspired and supported me throughout this research project.

Abstract

This book investigates Germany's real reasons for its involvement in the international Afghanistan intervention since 2001. The goal is to evaluate whether the main reason for the intervention is defending its security by combatting international terrorism as German authorities have been claiming or a decision that was made due to political and economic benefits. To follow this goal the research is based on an analysis of existing academic material together with official documents on the one hand and on findings coming from an empirical research trip to Afghanistan, where personal interviews with experts were conducted, on the other hand.

The main theoretical framework that underlies this research is Gramsci's contribution to Global Political Economy literature, which helps to explain structural reasons for Germany's decision to intervene in Afghanistan. Finally, the book concludes that Germany serves first of all its politic economic interests by its decision of intervening in Afghanistan. Although it also serves its basic security interests by strengthening its position in NATO and with regard on the changing security environment, it is not the security threat resulting from Islamic terrorism threat from Afghanistan, which can be used as the main reason for its intervention. Moreover, this research revealed that the source of Germany's decision to intervene in Afghanistan was a discrepancy between elites and the public. Consequently, this book suggests continuing to monitor whether the Afghanistan intervention with the support of Gramsci's theory about hegemony helped to implement consent in the civil society, which can be the basis that could drive also future German foreign policy decisions.

Introduction

> *"The security of the Federal Republic of Germany is also defended at the Hindukush" (Peter Struck, Former German Minister of Defence, 2002)*

Since the first years of Germany's intervention in Afghanistan, this official claim by Peter Struck has been frequently used in Germany to explain the main reason for Germany's involvement in this region. In recent years, the official explanation has focused more on stabilizing the whole region through international cooperation and rebuilding a sovereign Afghan state through mainly development cooperation. Is the explanation of decreasing the threat of international terrorism for Germany after more than 10 years of involvement justifiable or is Germany serving other national interests in Afghanistan? The objective of this project is to investigate Germany's real reasons for its involvement in the Afghanistan intervention. It will be evaluated whether the main reason for the intervention is defending its security by combatting international terrorism or a decision that was made due to political and economic benefits.

Information about terrorist organizations and their activities in Germany reveal that Germany was much safer before its involvement in Afghanistan than after 2001. Moreover, regional stability can serve economic and political interests, especially for developed countries in a capitalist system. Most obvious in Germany's efforts in Afghanistan is its role as a reliable ally of the US hegemony and its awareness of its security dependency from international alliances like NATO (North Atlantic Treaty Organization) in the new global world order. Certain gaps in the literature concerning these assumptions, make a detailed research on the reasoning behind Germany's intervention in Afghanistan necessary.

A) Background
From the beginning on, Germany was involved in the Afghanistan intervention. In the aftermath of the 9/11 attacks Germany assured to contribute within an intervention of the international community to fight against international terrorism. In 2001, the Bonn Agreement in Petersberg was arranged in Germany to agree on a strategy for the re-creation and reconstruction of an Afghan state. That year, the UN (United Nations) also decided to establish ISAF (International Security Assistance Force). Initially it purpose was assuring security for the Afghan government and the UN personnel. At the same time, Germany

decided not only to take part in the development aid programme for Afghanistan, but also to send its army (Bundeswehr) to Afghanistan both to contribute to the goal of a permanent stabilisation of Afghanistan and to combat international terrorism. Germany's contribution to the international mission in Afghanistan has increased steadily, both in the military area and in its civilian and reconstruction programmes. Germany has been the third biggest troop contributor as well as the third greatest financial donor within this NATO mission (Bundesregierung, 2013a; Bundesregierung, 2011).

Germany is mainly involved and responsible for the northern region around Mazar-i-Sharif and plays also an important role in Kabul and Kunduz. Moreover, it has been mainly responsible for the formation of the Afghan National Police (ANP) and invests up to 430 million euros each year for civil reconstruction purposes. In addition to that, around 5.000 German soldiers have been deployed in Afghanistan in each of the recent years. In general Germany enjoys a close relation to the Afghan government. Its role throughout the international mission can be described as an "honest broker" (Bundesregierung, 2011, p. 8), who was able to moderate in difficult situation of this intervention. Its efforts in form of contributions on various levels in Afghanistan have shown that it has been a staunch ally, who can play a leading position in an international intervention of the international community (Bundesregierung, 2011). Additionally, Germany committed itself to continue its support for Afghanistan, financially as one of the major donors for development aid and through the presence of NGOs, diplomats, instructors and specialists beyond the NATO troop withdrawal in 2014 (Bundesregierung, 2013a; Bundesregierung 2013b). A view on these activities raises the question of why Germany has made such an effort for Afghanistan, which this book will try to answer.

B) Structure & Research question
The overall research question in this book will be: Is Germany's intervention in Afghanistan driven by protecting its security from terrorism or by political-economic reasons?
All other sub-questions that follow can be linked to the overall research question and can be divided into two sections of identifying security or political-economic interests. To answer the main research question this book is divided into four chapters.

The first chapter will identify the official reasons for Germany's intervention in Afghanistan by analysing official governmental sources, which provide justifications for the German government's decision to be involved in the international mission in Afghanistan.

The second chapter will evaluate whether the main official argument of the German government, which was identified in the previous chapter (the protection against international terrorism), can be proven through available data. Therefore, this chapter will firstly determine whether the German intervention in Afghanistan did increase or decrease terrorism threat in Germany. Secondly, the link between failed states and terrorism will be discussed and consequently the impact of a possible failed Afghan state on Germany's security. Finally, Afghanistan's role in the context of the global War on Terror and how it has changed since the NATO intervention will be evaluated. The analysis will reveal that the Islamic terrorism threat in Germany has not decreased since Germany's intervention in Afghanistan and that the German government rather exaggerates the threat coming from it.

In the third part of this book it will be analysed why Germany justifies its intervention in Afghanistan particularly with the threat of international terrorism. In this context Germany's recent history will be discussed as well as its close connection to the NATO and the implications on Germany's foreign policy and its military. The change of its security strategy will be explained through the influence of an elitist consent about the desire of a powerful and influential German state in global world politics. The theoretical framework of Gramsci will be used to explain this process. This theory will demonstrate how Germany benefits from US hegemony.

Finally, the fourth chapter will analyse possible political-economic interests of Germany in Afghanistan. The determination of economic benefits from this intervention needs to be analysed with the due care to strengthen or disprove the hypothesis coming from the previous chapter. However, this evaluation is limited to determine the role of a cost-benefit analysis and geopolitical interests in Germany's decision to intervene in Afghanistan. In conclusion, the overall research question will be answered and the book will demonstrate that Germany's involvement in Afghanistan can be explained with the help of the applied theoretical framework.

C) Methodology & case study

The methodological approach to address the research questions is based upon a combination of a theoretical-empirical research strategy. This means that the findings coming from the book are based on the one hand on a theoretical research through an analysis of existing academic material together with official documents and on the other hand on an empirical research by the conduction of personal interviews with experts about the research topic.

The theoretical research required an in depth analysis and collection of relevant data from multiple primary (agreements, governmental official papers, public polls and reports of international institutions) and secondary sources (mainly books and journals). Due to the contemporary relevance for the German government and public, investigative newspaper articles will be used as well as Think-Tanks and German foundations, which are constantly drafting reports about the situation in Afghanistan and about Germany's foreign policy interests.

The discovered gaps in the literature about the topic and its sensitivity in the German political environment made an empirical research approach within this book necessary. Additionally, confidentiality and sensibility of this topic as well as the fact that information about economic and individual benefits or about security and intelligence are not publically accessible were some of the main limitations for this research. The researcher aimed to reduce those limitations and help to close the information gap within the literature about this topic by conducting interviews. However, the researcher decided to limit the empirical research to only one research trip to Afghanistan, mainly because of three reasons. Firstly, in contrast to the vast amount of accessible German literature about the research topic, accessible academic literature from Afghans, who have been on the ground, about this topic is limited. Secondly, the researcher's experience with personal interviews with German officials revealed that they usually do not contribute to new findings and rather point to already existent official documents online.

For this reason, a research trip to Kabul and Mazar-I-Sharif in Afghanistan was made from the 24th of June to the 9th of July 2013. The Ethic Code was applied throughout the research. During this research trip a number of high ranked Afghan and German current and former governmental representatives and bureaucrats, who are dealing with the international conflict in Afghanistan, were interviewed. The participants were selected according to their expertise about the research questions for this evaluation and their accessibility to the researcher. Within the participants there were very high-ranking Afghan officials like current governors or members of the Afghan government. Additionally, high representatives of the National Directorate of Security and the Ministry of Labor, Social Affairs, Martyrs & Disabled as well as the German embassy, members of the National Assembly, a former Afghan resistance fighter, members of the Ministry of Commerce and university professors were selected for personal interviews. This part occurred methodologically qualitative in open-ended semi-structured interviews and was conducted in the offices of the experts in Mazar-I-Sharif or Kabul.

As agreed with participants and to avoid any harm for the interviewees and their careers as well as having in mind the unstable political situation in Afghanistan the researcher decided that this book guarantees complete anonymity for all participants of the qualitative analysis. Therefore, the received information from this research trip will be used as background information for a better understanding of the research topic. However, if information from the interviews are quoted in this book the participant will not appear by name, but by his institutional affiliations.

In the analysis of political-economic interest the researcher had to consider several problematic aspects. In this regard this book acknowledges for instance the possibility to evaluate the development of trade business between Germany and its NATO allies since the intervention in Afghanistan in order to examine Germany's economic benefits from the intervention. However, to claim such an argument it would be also necessary to analyse also other aspects like e.g. development of world economy that could have affected the increase or decrease of trade business during that time period. Such an analysis would expand the capacity of this research and will consequently be ignored. A similar problem arose in the analysis of the security threat of international terrorism in Germany. When arguing that the intervention in Afghanistan has increased the terror threat in Germany it can only be proved relatively and not absolutely. This is because too many other aspects exist, which could have affected the terrorism threat but which are not measurable. For instance US military bases in Germany potentially increase the terrorism threat in Germany after the US call for the War on Terror. Even if Germany had not intervened in Afghanistan, attacks, which aim to target the US could harm Germans as collateral damage. Therefore, the claims coming from this book regarding the analysis of the security threat for Germany has to be understood more as a correlation between terrorism threat and Germany's intervention in Afghanistan, rather than a direct link between them.

These examples show that the selection of monetary and non-monetary benefits as well as conclusions resulting from the analysis of certain international correlations have to be made carefully. Due to the complexity and the limited capacity of the research a detailed analysis of intangible benefits like power and reputation will not be measured.

The focus on the case study of Afghanistan intends to illustrate an example of the general conflict of German foreign military intervention decisions within NATO missions. It is the best possible case study for that question, because it is the longest mission of the German military in the history of the German army (Bundeswehr) as well as highly relevant for Germany's international foreign policy ambitions. Germany's intervention in Afghanistan indicates the beginning of a key change of its military in an expeditionary force in order to meet global security challenges of the 21st century. It will be academically relevant, what role US hegemony plays in Germany's decision to intervene and connect it to Germany's sovereign national interests. This case study approach aims to find out what motivates a developed country with only limited security resources and power to intervene in a foreign conflict, from which it might not be immediately threatened. Moreover, the question whether security reasons or political-economic interests are dominating such a decision in Germany is not sufficiently discussed in the literature.

Finally, the Afghanistan case was selected by the researcher due to his personal German-Afghan cultural background and to his accessibility to first hand information on the ground.

D) Literature Review
Concerning Germany's intervention in Afghanistan an enormous amount of literature focuses on analysing and criticising Germany's military strategy and its role within NATOs ISAF mission in Afghanistan (Merz, 2007; Noetzel & Schreer, 2008; Belkin, 2010; Becker & Wulf, 2011). Opposed to that the literature review in this book will be divided in two aspects. On the one hand it will discuss literature that links Germany's intervention in Afghanistan to the terrorism threat and on the other hand it will point out those authors who link it to political-economic interests.

Former defence minister Peter Struck is known for his phrase: "The security of the Federal Republic of Germany is also defended at the Hindukush" (Struck in Becker & Wulf, 2011, p. 16). He was the first German official who claimed the link between Germany's security interests and Afghanistan in the public. Consequently, his statement started a debate about the validity of this claim, which is why a vast amount of secondary literature refers to this statement when analysing Germany's intervention in Afghanistan (Becker & Wulf, 2011; Meiers, 2010; Merz, 2007; Miko & Froehlich, 2004). However, Risse (2004, p. 29) argues that this statement has to be understood in a different context. He emphasises that Struck referred particularly to the necessity that Germany has to take responsibility, adapt its foreign policy strategies and contribute with its own resources to new challenges in a new environment of global security, where conflicts can be asymmetrical and are not anymore only authorised by states, but also by private actors. This book aims to clarify this disagreement in the literature.

To evaluate whether Germany's intervention has aimed at decreasing the terrorism threat for Germans the literature review needs to be broadened by general international terrorism literature. This enables the identification of whether the terrorism threat in Germany has increased or decreased since the intervention in Afghanistan.

Germany's involvement in Afghanistan started under the US called War on Terror. This US strategy focuses on defeating Al-Qaeda (AQ) and its affiliates, which also seems to be, at least officially, the main concern for Germany's security. Consequently, the broader international terrorism literature review will focus on Islamic influenced terrorism and AQ as its representative organization. Pape (2006, p. 47) claims that the ultimate aim of AQ ideology and its main driver is to end the Western occupation of the Arabian Peninsula. Having this aim in mind this book will determine whether Germany's involvement in Afghanistan is a driving force for provoking potential terror attacks in Germany. Such an assumed rationality of terrorist organizations, where terrorists want to provoke a desired response with their attacks is advocated and represented by Fromkin (1975). The Madrid bombings in 2004 exemplified politically motivated terrorism. Authors like Steinberg (2009) argue that there is evidence that these political reasons made Germany one of the highest ranked targets for Islamic influenced terrorists in the last years. The validity of this assumption will be examined in this book.

The claim made by German officials, making a connection between failed states and terrorism to justify military involvement in Afghanistan for the sake of Germany's security is mainly disproved by academic literature. Despite of the existence of an academic study, which claims that failed states are more likely to host international terrorism and commit transnational attacks (Piazza, 2008), the majority of authors in the literature deny a direct correlation (Pape, 2006; Simons & Tucker, 2007; Hehir, 2007).

Pape's research (2006, pp. 114-115) for instance reveals that only a minority of AQ suicide bombers were citizens of failed states, but more than 80% of attacks were committed by individuals from US allied countries. Nevertheless, his findings imply that those individuals could be radicalized by Germany's involvement in Afghanistan. Furthermore, several authors like Simons & Tucker (2007) or Hehir (2007) conclude with their empirical research that there is no correlation between state's level of failure and proliferation of terrorism. They argue that this link is rather misused by many Western countries to justify democracy promotion and interventions with state building initiatives. Simons & Tucker (2007, p. 388) offer many arguments for this hypothesis. They assert that a terrorist organization has many reasons to avoid failed states. A recruitment of a potential international terrorist from a developed society would pass easier border controls with a passport that does not arouse suspicion. Additionally, due to a familiarity with the environment the potential candidate would be better integrated in its developed "target" country compared to someone who comes from a failed state. They suggest that "in chaos not even terrorists are safe" (Simons & Tucker, 2007, p. 388). Furthermore, infrastructure and logistical problems would make it even more difficult for terrorist organizations to operate. When choosing settlement locations the main focus for terrorist organizations are socio-geographic aspects. The acceptability and support of a local population in a marginalized zone with a terrorist organization or with the ideology, delivers a much stronger protection for the terrorist organization than any failed state could assure (Simons & Tucker, 2007, pp. 397-398).

Moreover, the Afghanistan case seems to illustrate an example for Simons & Tucker (2007) findings. The reason why it became a harbour for AQ terrorists before 9/11 was not because it showed many typical characteristics of a failed state e.g. regarding its failed administrative capacity. Instead, it was rather decisive that the leaders of this country at that time, the Taliban, who have been also the dominant population in the essential border region between

Pakistan and Afghanistan, were able to guarantee essential support and stability to AQ (Hehir, 2007, pp. 318-319).

Furthermore, Afghanistan's role in the broader context of the War on Terror needs to be identified. If Germany's intervention shall be explained through an international terrorism threat coming from Afghanistan, it will need to be demonstrated that AQ and its affiliates still play an important role in this country and is using it for the recruitment of international terrorists. In the international terrorism literature the majority of authors distinguish between before 9/11 and post 9/11 when considering AQs role in Afghanistan. They underline a transformation from a small terrorist network with a base between the borders of Afghanistan and Pakistan into a radical ideology without a central authority that has inspired extremist Muslims around the world (Atwan, 2012; Burke, 2004; Pape, 2006). After the US destroyed the base of AQ in Afghanistan and killed a lot of members out of the inner circle, the remaining activists spread to different parts of the world (Atwan, 2012, p. 9). In addition to that, Wagner (in Tal, 2010, p. 119) emphasises studies in which the evaluation of the insurgents, who are fighting against the Afghan government and the international forces, reveals that only 10% of those insurgents identify themselves with an ideology of radical Islamism of the Taliban, which is similar to AQs ideology. These findings question the argument that the main reason for the Western involvement in Afghanistan is the fight against international terrorism and the AQ network. It therefore needs to be further analysed in this book.

The starting point in the literature to link political-economic interests as the main driver for the German intervention in Afghanistan can be identified in former Chancellor Gerhard Schröder's declaration on September 12th of 2001 to promise "unlimited solidarity" (Schröder, 2001) in the following of the 9/11 attacks to the United States.

Hein (2011, p. 137) indicates two reasons for Germany's intervention in Afghanistan. On the one hand he underlines Germany's national self-interests as well as its strive for becoming a powerful actor in political decisions about global security issues within the international community. On the other hand he emphasises the elimination of historical restrictions, which resulted from the World War II experience on Germany's sovereignty. He as well as Tal (2010) identify an elite consensus as the driving force behind the decision, which recognized that the international community expected a greater international security role from Germany after the Cold War. Germany has been able to assert this role through its military loyalty to NATO in the Afghanistan case (Hein, 2011). Belkin adds on that because of this action Germany expects "to be considered a credible partner, and maintain alliance security" (Belkin, 2010, p. 219). Other authors recognize also the World War II experience as a reason for Germany not to promote officially political-economic national interests to justify the mission in Afghanistan to the public (Belkin, 2010, p. 220) and agree with Hein (2011).

Many authors refer to the "Weißbuch" as the fundamental security strategy outline for Germany and assert that it illustrates perfectly Germany's adaption to the security challenges of the 21st century and a changing world order (Belkin, 2010; Hacke, 2012). Additionally, authors like Meyer (2007, pp. 22-23) remark that the Weißbuch legitimizes foreign military interventions for the sake of serving national interests; however it remains vague to define those national interests and prioritize them (Meyer, 2007, pp. 22-23). The book aims at clarifying to which degree economic interests can be considered as national interest with the Weißbuch, which could be legitimately defended even through a military intervention like for example in Afghanistan. In this context former president Horst Köhler was also highly criticized by the media, but simultaneously initiated a debate in the literature (Meiers, 2010; Becker & Wulf, 2011, p. 89; Hacke, 2012), because of his statement in an interview about Afghanistan. He referred to the hypothesis that it is also the job of Germany's military to defend national economic interests through foreign interventions in certain cases.

A deeper analysis of those economic German interests and benefits in Afghanistan lacks in the literature as well as a cost-benefit analysis. Most probably this is due to the fact that suggesting or assuming a hegemonic or imperialistic attitude as basis for German foreign policy decisions is still an absolute taboo subject, because of the already mentioned German history.
At least Destradi et al. (2012) mention economic benefits from regional stabilisation, nation building and geopolitical interests (Baraki in Tal, 2010, p. 36) in Afghanistan. However, an analysis of the actions that were taken on the ground and the strategies of governmental decision makers reveal that a strategy that prioritize nation building was never followed within the US led war in Afghanistan (Rashid, 2009; Woodward, 2010; Hassan & Hammond, 2011). Nevertheless, there are some authors who discuss the costs of the German intervention in Afghanistan (DIW, 2010; Miko & Frohelich; 2004, Tal, 2010). In conclusion, neither on

Germany's individual economic benefits nor on benefiting actors from the war in Afghanistan the literature does provide enough material.

One part of this book will aim at closing the gap in the literature and discover economic benefits for Germany from its mission in Afghanistan. Research aspects will include an analysis of possible benefits from trading or accessing natural resources through its mission in Afghanistan. Apart from that this book will not position itself in the same line with the mentioned authors about providing Germany's reasons for intervening in Afghanistan. Instead it will combine the different paths in the literature and define which role the terrorism threat plays in the decision to be involved in Afghanistan as well as determine the role of NATO connected with political-economic interests for the explanation of this foreign policy decision. Even if some authors try to use such a multiple interest approach to evaluate Germany's involvement in Afghanistan (Keller, 2009; Tal, 2010; Risse, 2004), none of them captures the whole picture of this complex decision and uses a Global Political Economy framework to deal with it, as this book will aim at doing.

E) Theoretical Framework

The theoretical framework will be applied to evaluate two hypotheses, which the literature review revealed. Firstly, that the terrorism threat in Germany has rather increased than decreased through the intervention in Afghanistan, even though it was used as the main reason by governmental officials, mainly to exaggerate the security threat and justify the war. Secondly, to keep on benefiting from the US hegemonic system and remaining a global political power, Germany was not forced to be involved in Afghanistan, but rather encouraged, because it holds the opinion to serve its own national interests with the decision.

Firstly, the theoretical approach of the foreign policy analysis of Alden & Aran (2012) will be applied to identify the decision-making process that led to Germany's intervention in Afghanistan. This includes a behaviouristic approach, where the psychological environment, perceptions of individual actors and the structures of foreign policy (Alden & Aran, 2012, p. 20) will be taken into account. Secondly, assumptions from realist authors like Morgenthau (2006) about national interests and the striving for state security and power will serve as a basis for developing main arguments in this book. However, a realist theoretical framework seems to be incapable of capturing the complexity of this research topic. Consequently,

Gramsci's contribution to Global Political Economy literature will be essential to complement the theoretical framework for the research and explain structural reasons for Germany's decision to intervene in Afghanistan. Gramsci's theory will help to emphasize the hypothesis that the reasons for Germany's intervention in Afghanistan were neither solely security reasons nor pure economic interests. Instead it will help to connect both areas through its theory.

In detail Gramsci's understanding of hegemony, which emphasises a combination of "consent and coercion for hegemony" (Cox, 1983, p. 164), where the hegemon creates a world order which matches common interests of secondary states will be applied to discover political-economic benefits that Germany receives because of its intervention in Afghanistan. The provision of security as a public good could be an example of such a benefit. To apply this theory the German state has to be redefined and institutions and elites have to be included in the enlarged state definition. Moreover, the NATO's role as an international institution (IO), which works as a tool for the hegemon, has to be evaluated. According to Gramsci, with the help of IOs the hegemon can implement and legitimize the "rules of the game" and connect elites between states, which will recognize that they would benefit of the established world order (Cox, 1983, pp. 171-172). Germany's benefits from being part of such a major international foreign policy mission like the one in Afghanistan have to be discussed in the context of the dynamics and processes of the world order.

1. Analysis of Germany's official story - a security threat from Afghanistan

To analyse Germany's motives for being involved in Afghanistan this book will start by discussing the official arguments, interests and aims of the German government regarding the initiative of Germany's military intervention in Afghanistan. Furthermore, it addresses its current reasons for being still engaged in that country. Especially, primary literature will be used both to demonstrate Germany's official interests in Afghanistan and to reveal whether the justifications have changed since the beginning of the intervention in 2001.

According to the German government, currently the aim and focus of Germany's involvement in Afghanistan lies in the reconstruction of Afghanistan and the advising of Afghan security forces. This period is driven by the already started transition of security responsibility from the international forces to the Afghan forces (Bundesregierung, 2013b). According to the US and NATO strategy in Afghanistan the security transition will be completed by the end of 2014. Then, the great majority of foreign forces will be withdrawn from Afghanistan and the few thousands remaining forces will change their responsibility from combat to support (Obama, 2009). The German government explains its Afghanistan policy by dividing the German mission in Afghanistan into four areas: "Development cooperation, protection of the development, construction of the police and transition of security responsibility" (Bundesregierung, 2013a). The Bundeswehr underlines that Germany is involved in Afghanistan as part of the international community and that its priority in this mission is to prevent Afghanistan becoming again a safe haven for international terrorists (Bundeswehr, 2013; Senior member of the German Embassy Kabul, Interview, 2013). Furthermore, the Ministry of Defence summarizes that from the beginning of the intervention in Afghanistan it has been basically "all about three issues: about our own security, those of our allies and about the future of Afghanistan" (Bundesministerium der Verteidigung, 2013).

The point of defending Germany's own security made by the Ministry of Defence can be linked to the publicly well known sentence of former Minster of Defence Peter Struck at the beginning of the intervention in Afghanistan to explain the main reason for Germany's mission (see section D on p. 10). The already mentioned disagreement in the literature about the interpretation of this statement can be clarified on a closer examination of the context of this speech in combination with other speeches and actions of Peter Struck during this time period as the Minister of Defence in Germany.

The first time he made this statement was in a discussion about the further development of the Bundeswehr. It seems obvious that he wanted to emphasize that a structural change of the Bundeswehr is necessary to meet today's security challenges. Due to the fact that at that time his ministry was working on a reformation of the guidelines to open up the political possibilities to the use of German forces for international interventions he had a self-interest in using the intervention in Afghanistan as an ideal for the necessity of future German security contributions in international interventions. According to Peter Struck, a traditional national defence at national boarders is unlikely and is not enough in a globalised world where threats to the homeland can arise from all over the world without regional or local limitation. To illustrate this change in a new environment of global security he mentioned Germany's intervention in Afghanistan (Struck, 2002 b). Directly after his statement in his speech he goes on to claim that terrorist organizations like AQ or the Taliban are able to carry out terrorist attacks on countries like Germany due to safe havens, like Afghanistan before 2001 (Struck, 2002 a).

Additionally, in an interview about the German intervention in Afghanistan he makes a clear connection between failed states and the increase of terrorism and explains that in order to prevent this from happening German troops are engaged in Afghanistan (SPIEGEL, 2009). The validity of this assumption of an existing link between terrorism and failed states as well as of the argument of decreasing terrorism threat in Germany with the intervention in Afghanistan will be examined later in this book. However, the above mentioned statements finally clarify Struck's intentions with his famous statement about Afghanistan.

Probably the most important official document that deals with Germany's intervention in Afghanistan is the "progress report". Since 2010, it is published annually by the German government in cooperation with all ministries who are involved in Afghanistan to inform the Bundestag (Lower house of Parliament) about Germany's efforts as well as about the current situation for the people in Afghanistan and the international community. The reports are usually divided in three areas: security, governance and development. The progress report 2011 says "our aim still is that there will never be a threat coming from Afghanistan to the world again" (Bundesregierung, 2011, p. 4). This suggests that for Germany one of its main goals and interests of preventing another 9/11 attack and defeating international terrorism in Afghanistan has not changed since the beginning of the intervention.

However, the progress report also emphasises that the reasons for this goal rely both on Germany's own security interests and on Germany's solidarity towards the US immediately after 9/11 (see also "unlimited solidarity" on p. 12). It goes on to assert that the focus in the Afghanistan policy has to shift from military support towards development and political aid to assure that Afghanistan is able to become a sovereign and responsible state to enable it, to contribute to peace and regional stability in the future (Bundesregierung, 2011, p. 7; Senior member of the German Embassy Kabul, Interview, 2013). The question of the price and the beneficiaries of that stability will be discussed in the next chapter. Additionally, the progress report mentions that apart from the threat of Islamic terrorism, transnational drug trafficking and the presence of nuclear weapons in India and Pakistan are the reason why the region around Afghanistan affects the world's security and stability. "This is the most important reason why the international community is involved so extensively over there" (Bundesregierung, 2011, p. 50). The importance of this geopolitical argument will be further evaluated during the analysis of Germany's political-economic interests in the last chapter.

In contrast to the Afghanistan strategy in 2001, in 2011, the international community started to distinguish between Taliban and AQ in order to decrease UN sanctions against the Taliban, without changing them for AQ. It also made peace talks between them and the Afghan government possible. Germany played a major role in achieving this strategic realignment (Bundesregierung, 2011, p. 49). Additionally, following newspaper articles (i.e. Herwartz, 2012) and the development of public appearances from German Defence Ministers since 2001, it becomes obvious that in recent years Germany as well as the international community gave their ambition to establish a kind of Western democracy in Afghanistan as promised at the beginning of the intervention up. Instead, the focus of the intervention shifted more towards the aspect of regional stability.

To conclude Germany's official version of its involvement in Afghanistan, this research will analyse Germany's own assessment since the intervention. In general, Germany claims that it has been successful in Afghanistan, even if it admits that in the future, a lot of work still needs to be done. Moreover, it indicates areas for improvement (Senior member of the German Embassy Kabul, Interview, 2013; Bundesregierung, 2011). According to the German government, the main threat for the international community, AQ and Islamic extremism coming from Afghanistan, were contained. The Taliban government collapsed and Osama Bin Laden is dead (Bundesregierung, 2011, p. 50). In addition to that, in the end of 2014, the transition of security responsibility to the Afghan forces will be completed and the promised goal to establish an army of 352.000 Afghans serving within the Afghan National Security Forces (ANSF) is almost reached (Bundesregierung, 2013b, p. 12).

Moreover, Germany especially highlights its achievements in cooperation with the efforts of the international community in the areas of humanitarian aid and reconstruction. It asserts its effort for Afghanistan's education system by building schools and universities. It also highlights the accessibility to social benefits, particularly for women, due to for example a reformed health system, the reconstruction of infrastructure by building new roads and provision of alternative transportation routes (Bundesregierung, 2013b; Senior member of the German Embassy Kabul, Interview, 2013).

The following chapter will evaluate the validity of the main claims of the German government about the reasons for its intervention in Afghanistan and discuss the related topics academically, especially by using secondary literature.

2. Examination of Germany's hypothesis

As demonstrated above the most dominant reason in the official debate about Germany's reasons for intervening and engaging in Afghanistan has been to combat international terrorism for the sake of Germany's own security, which implies the aim of decreasing the threat of terror attacks in Germany. After a clarification about definitions that will be used in this book and an introduction into the AQ organization the claims made by the German government will be examined in detail.

2.1. International Terrorism
There is no universally accepted legal or academic consensus about the definition of terrorism. Nevertheless, different authors underline common aspects. The use of violence by a non state-actor to create fear for a political aim can be identified as the main characteristic (Laqueur, 1996, p. 24; Lutz & Lutz, 2008, p. 9; Shea, 2009; Bellamy, 2008, p. 28). In addition to that, Shea (2009) points out that the act has to carry symbolic value as well as follow the goal to mobilize the terrorist's community. Bellamy (2008, p. 28) includes that civilians have to be the target. However, only Fromkin underlines that "the uniqueness of the strategy lies in this: that it achieves its goal not through its acts but through the response to its acts" (Fromkin, 1975, p. 692). Fromkin's notion implies the major power of terrorism as well as its main weakness due to its passive role in the dependence from the reaction of the state (See section D on p. 10). This essay agrees with the validity of these definitions and considers terrorism as international terrorism when it is practised in foreign countries by terrorists who are not native to that country.

For this book the security threat for Germany in the context of the intervention in Afghanistan and the aftermath of 9/11 can be narrowed down to Islamic terrorism or Islamic extremism. In the past, when defining Islamic extremism the focus lay on strict interpretations of Islamic teaching especially, those from the Quran or from Hadiths of the prophet Muhammad. During that time, many scholars had referred to the promotion and expansion of Islam through Jihad and the implementation of Sharia Law in Islamic societies. In the contemporary debate the term stands for a conservative view of Islamic ideology, which aims to reconstruct a society as it was during Muhammad's period. Here the Islamic religion plays the central role and the state and society are subordinated because of the introduction of the Sharia law, which consequently means for the majority also stopping and combating the influence of non-

Islamic states in Muslim lands (Farmer, 2007). The official reason why the US started the intervention in Afghanistan in 2001 was to defeat AQ. As probably the biggest and most famous Islamic terrorist organization AQ and its affiliates underlie such an Islamic extremist believe and will be used in the context of the war in Afghanistan as the main representative terrorist organization in this book.

2.2. AQ & Taliban
According to the former US Director of the Central Intelligence Agency (CIA) Leon Panetta, in 2010 the estimated number of AQ fighters in Afghanistan was about 50-100 (Rollins, 2011, p. 8). Wagner (in Tal, 2010, p. 119) adds on that only ten percent of the Afghan insurgency are following extremist Islamist ideologies. Comparing this relatively low number with other states, where AQ and its affiliates represent a major security threat like for example currently in Yemen, Pakistan, Iraq or Syria, arises the following question: If the international community's main priority in Afghanistan is to combat international terrorism why is an international intervention in those other countries missing? This research does not question that Afghanistan was a safe haven for AQ terrorists in 2001. Nevertheless, it argues that since the military intervention in Afghanistan, the centre for Islamic terrorists has changed to other countries, where AQ cells and associates are located. At the moment AQ like-minded cells operate in over 70 states (Rollins, 2011, summary) and its stronghold seems to be in Yemen (Sydow, 2013) and especially in Pakistan, owing to the fact that in one way or the other every Islamic motivated attack in Europe, America and Asia can be directly or indirectly traced back to Pakistan (Former high representative of the National Directorate of Security, Interview, 2013).

The wrong perception of Afghanistan's role and weight in the context of global Islamic terrorism originates partly in the media's misunderstanding of the connection between the Afghan Taliban and AQ, which led to the exaggeration of the terrorism threat coming from Afghanistan since 2001. Especially at the beginning of the intervention in Afghanistan many reports did not distinguish between AQ and the Taliban. However, "Afghans have not been involved in international terrorism, nor have the Afghan Taliban adopted the internationalist jihadi rhetoric of affiliates of al-Qaeda" (Van Linschoten & Kuehn, 2011, p. 4). Moreover, even currently, internal armed conflicts between tribes, warlords or different ethnic groups are often illustrated as terror attacks from AQ or the Taliban (Former Mujahideen fighter,

Interview, 2013; High representative governing northern Afghanistan, Interview, 2013). This research will only focus on the Afghan Taliban and will not discuss further the reasoning and role of the Pakistani Taliban in this conflict, which is different to the one of the Afghan Taliban and has more in common with AQ's ideology (Barett, 2008, summary).

The difference between Afghan Taliban and AQ is very clear. Van Linschoten & Kuehn (2011) assert that the Taliban appeared first during the time of the war against the Soviets where they were "members of fronts composed of religious students (Taliban) that formed most of the fighters of the two madrasa-based parties of the Afghan resistance" (Van Linschoten & Kuehn, 2011, p. 3). Furthermore, van Linschoten & Kuehn go on to argue that the Taliban even discussed to join the political process of the new Afghan government in the aftermath of 2001. However, the counter-terrorism strategy of the US, which considered the Taliban as enemies and promoted the idea of connection and cooperation between AQ and Taliban, prevented a national reconciliation process from happening in Afghanistan. Consequently, the Afghan Taliban decided to start an insurgency for two reasons: On the one hand to assure their own survival and on the other hand to fight against the foreign occupation of Afghanistan. In contrast to the AQ ideology the Taliban "do not see themselves in a conflict that extends beyond the borders of Afghanistan" (Van Linschoten & Kuehn, 2011, p. 8; Former Mujahideen fighter, Interview, 2013). For this reason, "Al-Qaeda and the Afghan Taliban remain two distinct groups, with different membership, agendas, ideologies, and objectives" (Van Linschoten & Kuehn, 2011, p. 4). Even if it is possible that apart from their own ideology some of the Afghan Taliban might sympathize also with the AQ ideology, their clear separation from AQ and the Pakistani Taliban relativizes the terrorism threat coming from Afghanistan.

2.3. Analysis of available terrorism data
To get an impression of the intensity of Islamic terrorism threat in Europe, since 2006, Europol publishes annually its EU terrorism situation and Trend report. The report revealed that Separatist Terrorists committed 70% of attacks in the EU in 2012 followed by left-wing terrorists who were responsible for around 8% of attacks (Europol, 2013, p. 9). Opposed to that religiously inspired terrorism killed 8 people in 6 attacks in 2012, which represented about 3% of the total amount of committed terrorist attacks in that year in Europe (Europol, 2013, p. 42). However, with 159 arrests in Europe, 6 out of them in Germany, religiously

inspired terrorists represented 30% of arrested terrorists in 2012 in Europe (Europol, 2013, p. 42). Nevertheless, the analysis of terrorist attacks in Europe during 2007-2012 reveals that in average less than 1% of terrorist attacks have been committed by Islamic extremists (Europol, 2007-2013).

This data seems to imply that the terrorism threat coming from Islamic terrorism does not represent the main terrorism threat for European countries like Germany and that the threat has been inflated compared to the reality. But despite of this, it also has to be considered in this terrorism threat assessment that if one of these prevented Islamic terrorist plans, which is demonstrated partly through the number of arrested terrorists, had been actually committed it would have a major effect on the whole statistic. Moreover, left-wing terrorism as well as Separate terrorism are usually national actors and are consequently much more difficult to influence through international actions than Islamic terrorists, who often operate internationally. Nevertheless, the evaluation of this data suggests that European countries should give a higher priority to combat national terrorism threats, rather than to focus only on the international terrorism threat through the threat of Islamic terrorism.

The German Federal Ministry of the Interior identifies a change of Islamic terror threat for Germany and claims that, "since 2001 we have become from a transit country to one of the target countries for international terrorism" (Bundesministerium des Inneren, 2013). The identification of this change is interesting due to the fact that it is brought forward by an official German body. This implies that Islamic terrorism threat for Germany has risen dramatically since 2001. Nevertheless, the main reason for this change is given to the attacks of 9/11 and the appearance of AQ as an international terrorist organization and has not been connected at all to the German intervention in Afghanistan. However, the report of the German Office of the Protection of the German Constitution states that the majority of Islamic terrorist organizations in Germany justify their activity in Germany with the German participation in the combat against Islamic terrorism and particularly with Germany's intervention in Afghanistan (Bundesamt für Verfassungsschutz, 2010, p. 202). Consequently, the German Federal Ministry of the Interior links Germany's intervention in Afghanistan directly to an increase of Islamic terrorism threat in Germany.

A further indication for the increase of Islamic terror threat for Germany is the evaluation of the data, of the reports of the German Office for the Protection of the Constitution. According to those reports, Islamic extremists as well as Islamic organizations have risen almost constantly each year in Germany since 2001; from 31.000 people and 20 identified organizations in 2000 (Bundesamt für Verfassungsschutz, 2001, p. 197) to 38.000 people (+19 %) and 30 organizations (+33%) in 2011 (Bundesamt für Verfassungsscutz, 2011, p. 225).

The German Federal Ministry of Interior (Bundesministerium des Inneren, 2013) asserts that Islamic terrorism is still threatening Germany's security and emphasises that through the quality of the German security services as well as through international cooperation with foreign intelligence services it has been possible to prevent major planned attacks from Islamic terrorists in Germany in recent years. Currently, 100 people in Germany are estimated to be potential Islamic extremists, who could be able to carry out an attack in Germany. Some of those seem suspicious to the German authorities because they are accused of having been trained in terror camps in the border region of Afghanistan and Pakistan (Bundesministerium des Inneren, 2013). Nevertheless, many cases in the past, in which suspected people proved their innocence like in Guantanamo, indicate that numbers given by international authorities about potential international terrorists remain ambiguous.

In the majority of those cases the German security services were not able to recognize a link between an international terrorist network like AQ and the suspect. Although those potential terrorists seem to act for the sake of their own will or in small groups of like-minded people, they have in common that they often orientate themselves at the AQ ideology (see section D) and were raised or born in European countries (Bundesamt für Verfassungsschutz, 2010, p. 203). These Islamic extremists, who represent a major group that threatens Germany's security, arise the question of how the intervention in Afghanistan is able to defend Germany's security if those so called "lone wolves" do have nothing to do with the potential international terrorists in Afghanistan?

Finally, the already mentioned thesis of former Defence Minister Struck that a failed Afghan state would increase Islamic terrorism threat in Germany needs to be discussed. Instead of a universal definition of a failed state only a debate about the form of such a definition exist. The main problem is the exact determination about the moment of calling a country failed state. Due to the fact that a detailed definition is irrelevant for this book, it will be generally characterized as a state that fails in its social, political and economic capacity. As discussed in the literature review, although many characteristics of a failed state facilitate international terrorism in a failed state (Piazza, 2008), from an academic perspective the majority of authors deny convincingly that a direct correlation between failed states and international terrorism does exist (see section D on p. 11). A weak state which is able to provide basic infrastructure, local support and security for the ideology of the terrorist organization, good access to the outside world and with no monitoring of a foreign intervention seems to be more attractive as a location for an international terrorist organization. In practise, the fact that captured AQ documents reveal that in the 90s "Somalia was too failed even for AQ" (Foreign Policy, 2009) indicates the validity of the above mentioned characteristics.

In conclusion, the hypothesis that a failed Afghan state would increase the international terrorism threat for the rest of the world can become true under certain conditions. However, one has to put this statement into perspective. On the one hand the question whether Afghanistan is already a failed state demonstrates the difficulty of this assumption and on the other hand the main reason for international terrorist organizations for the decision to settle in the region will not be the level of state failure, but rather the case of foreign intervention will stay in their focus when deciding to move back to Afghanistan. Nevertheless, in contrast to these findings a very experienced member of the Afghan National Directorate of Security asserts that the withdrawal of the international forces in Afghanistan in the end of 2014 will increase destabilization of Afghanistan as well as increase international terrorism (High representative of the National Directorate of Security, Interview, 2013). However, through US military bases as well as a number of foreign troops, who will focus on supporting the ANSF and continue hunting for international terrorists in this region, most probably between 9.000 and 20.000 NATO troops will stay in Afghanistan. The decision about the exact amount has not been made yet (Starvidris, 2013). This perspective seems rather unattractive for a potential settlement location for international terrorists, even if the political- economic and social situation of the country will worsen.

2.4. Reassessment of the German story

As discussed in the previous chapter, the German government has the opinion that in general the international intervention has been successful. Particularly, the success in the area of security, with the efforts against international terrorism and AQ, as well as the transition of security responsibility to the Afghan forces is underlined. The literature review revealed (see section D on p. 12) that it is true that the AQ central network, which was based in Afghanistan, before 2001 was quickly destroyed because of the international intervention. Many high leading members have been killed or captured. Nonetheless, this did not lead to a decrease of Islamic terror threat for the international community and an absent of a repetition of a terror attack like 9/11 does not mean that international terrorism is contained by now. It demonstrates that in times of intelligence cooperation and violations of privacy for data collection states are more effective in uncovering and preventing planned attacks than ever before. The evaluated data reveals that the AQ ideology has spread to millions of Muslims around the world. Thus, instead of one safe haven in Afghanistan, there exist several other states in which Islamic terrorists have a stronghold and that consequently the threat of terroristic attacks by Islamists is higher than before 9/11. Germany is still a top target for them and is also threatened by the increased number of homegrown Islamic extremists in recent years.

To determine whether the security situation in Afghanistan has been improved since the intervention in 2001 an analysis of fatalities from NATO and ISAF forces as well as an overview of the development of civilian deaths in Afghanistan becomes necessary. The number of fatalities of foreign troops in Afghanistan has steadily increased since 2001 with a peak of 711 fatalities in 2010 and has been decreased to 402 causalities in 2012 (Icasualities, 2013). The development of civilian deaths in Afghanistan looks similar. The number has constantly risen from 1500 civilian deaths in 2007 and doubled with 3000 civilian deaths in the last two years (United Nations Assistant Mission in Afghanistan, 2013).

This data about the security situation in Afghanistan does not suggest a success of the foreign intervention in Afghanistan and questions highly the assumption of an improved security situation as well as a safe environment for a responsible security transition as claimed by the international forces. The claim that the ANSF will be able to be responsible for its own security by the end of 2014 seems to be more of a desire of NATO than a fact. Karlekar (2012, p. 272) shares those doubts and argues that according to the US Counter Insurgency Strategy it requires an ANSF of about 700.000 in order to secure Afghanistan. However, the indicated target size for ANSF is only 352.000, which will be reached by the end of 2014 (Bundesregierung, 2013b). Moreover, it is planned to reduce the size of the ANSF to 228.500 by 2017. Apart from the negative consequences on the internal Afghan security of such a reduction, the estimated costs to maintain such a force at such a level beyond 2017 are around four billion USD. The Afghan government will not be able to contribute such an amount. Therefore, the Afghan government will remain dependant on the contributions of the international community to balance the necessary budget, although NATO members have not agreed on how to collect this money and have been remaining short in their promises of contributions to Afghanistan throughout the whole intervention (Coffey, 2013; Karlekar, 2012 pp. 273-274).

The assessment of the validity of Germany's claims regarding what has been achieved by the intervention in Afghanistan revealed that there is a gap between the reality and Germany's assessment. Furthermore, the above mentioned facts also raise the question why the international community wants to withdraw its troops from Afghanistan in 2014 although the main goal of assuring security and stability in Afghanistan will not be achieved? Due to the limitations of this research project this question will not be answered.

In conclusion, the protection of Germany's own security as the main reason for Germany's intervention in Afghanistan is highly doubted. The Islamic terrorism threat analysis for Germany revealed that the threat has not decreased since the intervention in 2001 in Germany. The available data rather serves as a basis to assume that it has dramatically risen due to the fact that the AQ ideology is followed by as many Muslims as never before. The number of extremist Islamic organizations and their members in Germany has risen and the problem of homegrown Islamic terrorists appeared.

Nevertheless, the threat coming from Afghanistan and its influence on Germany's own security still has to be put into perspective. The number of international terrorists like AQ fighters in Afghanistan is very low at the moment and the Afghan Taliban are not primary fighting for reasons, which go beyond the boarders of Afghanistan. Additionally, the data from Europol reveals that even if Islamic terrorism threatens European countries, it can be calculated and its relevance to the security of European people is overestimated by the society and in the public debate.

Furthermore, a analysis of the number of arrested people and fatalities because of attacks of Islamic terrorists rather seem to imply that the intelligence services are able to contain the threat at the moment. It further suggests that terrorists who are motivated by other reasons than religion like separatists or left-wings are much more dangerous for the security of

European people. Finally, data about the intervention in Afghanistan revealed that the security situation is still unstable and that Germany and its NATO allies have not been able to meet their major security goals in Afghanistan.

The analysis showed that Germany did not decrease the threat through the intervention. On the contrary, it is more likely that Germany's actions heightened the risks of Islamic terrorism in Germany. This conclusion raises the question of why the German government uses the threat of international terrorism and the protection of its own security as the main reason for the intervention in Afghanistan. Either Germany has never known about the real impact of its intervention or there exists another explanation for it, which shall not be promoted publically. This research will make a case for the latter and discuss the reasons for it.

3. Analysis of the reasons for the German approach

In this section, the book will argue that the construction or rather exaggeration of the Islamic terror threat by the German government helped Germany justify its intervention in Afghanistan without loosing public support. This part will highlight long-term structural benefits from Germany's intervention and argue that the intention was to serve its national interests.

3.1. Afghanistan – an opportunity to implement an elitist consent
To understand Germany's military structure and the public opinion both about security questions and the desired role of the Bundeswehr, every analysis needs to begin with the conclusions Germany has drawn from starting two world wars. Regarding the structure of its army, Germany restricted its military actions only to (self-) defence, which can be seen in the German Constitution (Bundesministerium der Justiz, 2013), and internalized the principles of "never alone" and "never again" (Hamann in Jaberg et al., 2009, p. 56). This has been the basis for having used its military predominately in joint international missions and also explains why German military activities have focused particularly on humanitarian assistance and peacekeeping missions since the Post-Cold War era. "As a result the German Armed Forces' deployments came to be seen in Germany as armed development aid rather than genuine military operations" (Merz, 2007, p. 3).

During the Cold War period the Bundeswehr was notably used for deterrence purposes (von Bredow, 2011, p. 2). Germany rather contributed financially instead of militarily to international interventions. The end of the Cold War changed the security environment. At that point NATO started to overthink its strategy and to restructure its military resources to adapt to new global security challenges. New tasks like solving crises and conflict appeared on NATO's agenda and simultaneously the expectations of a German military involvement in international cooperation rose (Gareis & Nolte in Jaberg et al, 2009, pp. 30-31). Influenced by those new developments, Germany started to redefine its role as a military actor as well. Similar to NATO's new processes Germany started to smooth the way for the transformation of its army from an army for national defence purposes to an expeditionary force (Haid in Tal, 2010, p. 90; Merz, 2007, p. 3).

The first ones promoting this idea were especially German elites and the two main German policy Think-Tanks *Wissenschaft und Politik* (SWP) and Deutsche *Gesellschaft für Auswärtige Politik* (DGAP), who started arguing in 1990 that "national interests need to receive a greater consideration in German Foreign and Security Policy" (Meyer, 2007, p. 8). For the purpose of simplification and to avoid a debate about the definition of elites, the definition of elites in Germany in this book shall include the "power elite" (Domhoff, 2005). The power elite influences governmental decisions according to own interests and can be identified with an extremely overrepresentation as certain corporate owners, CEOs of multinational companies and people in key positions in non-profit Organizations, in the government, in foundations or in Think-Tanks. In addition to that, Hartmann (2004) also includes influential attorneys, professors and journalists in its definition of a "society elite", which shall also be considered in the elite definition of this research.

The results of the above mentioned elitist policy promotion can be observed in the guidelines of the Ministry of Defence in 1992. In these guidelines it seems as if the maintenance of a capitalist or neo-liberal world order became also a German national interest and has been since then an element of its security policy (Bundesministerium der Verteidigung, 1992). Those official guidelines, which serve as an orientation for the Bundeswehr, emphasize the importance of the security umbrella through Germany's collaboration with NATO and include in the understanding of Germany's security interests: "the maintenance of world trade and the unhindered access to markets and resources in the whole world within a framework of a fair world economic system" (Bundesministerium der Verteidigung, 1992).

In the following, "since the country's highest court decided in 1994 that troop deployments in foreign countries resulting from its membership in multilateral organizations were constitutional, the German Armed Forces have participated in UN, NATO and European Union (EU) missions, notably in the Balkans and in Africa" (Merz, 2007, p. 2). From that point until today Germany has been able to justify foreign military interventions within multilateral institutions trough the link of national interests and security policy.

The final step in implementing this expanded area of responsibility for the Bundeswehr can be found in the Weißbuch, which is the official security policy manual for Germany until today. It is the latest version and was published in 2006 by the German ministry of defence. The Weißbuch demonstrates very well the transformation of Germanys foreign policy ambitions. It explains why the new security environment makes it to expand the Bundeswehr's site of operation to a global one. It also includes economic interests besides other German security interests in its duties. Additionally, it emphasises close relations to the US, which represents the basis for Germany's own security (Bundesministerium der Verteidigung, 2006, p. 24). However, by using vague terms it fails to name the exact conditions under which Germany shall deploy its army and consequently remains open to interpretations of the German government for its decisions to use military forces (Bundesministerium der Verteidigung, 2006).

Behind this strategic outline for Germany's foreign policy seems to be the idea of German elites that only military participation assures the right to participate in the decision-making process within a concert of world powers under US hegemony. However, the German public has always been mistrustful towards this policy shift (Merz, 2007, p. 2). For this reason, it has been an act of balance for German governments between fulfilling expectations of its allies as well as elitist institutions and not loosing the support in the national parliament and public, where the majority would still like to avoid German foreign military interventions (Merz, 2007; Gareis & Nolte in Jaberg et al, p. 41). A population survey in Germany in 2009 revealed that a vast majority of more than 90 percent of the participants, do not have comprehensive knowledge about any of the Bundeswehr's current out of area missions (von Bredow, 2011, pp. 3-4). Furthermore, "when asked about the priorities of Germany's foreign and security policy, the most prominent [five] issues and goals, with high degrees of concurrence among Germans, are: (1) disaster relief, (2) environment protection (3) secure peace and (4) Germany's supply of energy and raw materials [as well as] (5) enhance respect for human rights" (von Bredow, 2011, p. 4).

Another good example for this discrepancy between German elites and citizens is Germany's military intervention in Afghanistan. After Germany's military contribution in a major NATO intervention in Kosovo in the end of the 90s, which was justified with humanitarian aspects, the ISAF mission in Afghanistan seemed to be a good opportunity to balance further German ambitions: On the one hand to be one of the leading states in political decisions and on the other hand to improve and extend its international image in the eyes of its allies without loosing the support of its sceptical electorate (Tal, 2010; Merz, 2007; von Bredow, 2011).

The ISAF mission was seen as a peaceful mission that focused on providing the security for the new Afghan government and the international aid workers which was necessary to reconstruct a future for Afghanistan. Due to this idea of protection of Afghan welfare combined with Germany's further claim to defend its own security with the intervention in Afghanistan, the majority of the German public supported this military decision. This argument can be supported by a population survey of *Infratest Dimap*, which revealed that at the beginning of the Afghanistan intervention 62% of the German population supported the ISAF mission. However, the same survey reveals also that between 2002-2009 the dissatisfaction of the public about Germany's mission in Afghanistan has continuously grown every year. The number of those, who wanted the mission to continue in 2009 dropped to only 17%, (von Bredow, 2011, p. 5). In contrast to that, the support of the German government towards the Afghanistan mission has been much more stable. Since 2001, a stable majority in three successive German governments has supported the Afghanistan mission throughout the years. Moreover, "Germany has [even] been gradually extending its engagement since 2001" (Merz, 2007, p. 7).

This different opinion about Germany's mission in Afghanistan demonstrates that "a gap has opened between the attitude of political elites and the German population" (von Bredow, 2011, p. 5). By providing special military equipment like the Tornado aircrafts or deploying covert special forces like the Kommando Spezialkräfte (KSK) (Merz, 2007, p. 7) and gradually taking the lead in some NATO operations, Germany has been able to demonstrate that it has the will as well as the capacity to contribute militarily in an international intervention. Nonetheless, the time of these commitments imply that Germany is using a passive military strategy and has usually made these contributions to particularly reduce the pressure and meet the expectations coming from its NATO allies and partners. This explains also why Germany's commitment in Afghanistan dramatically increased in 2003, directly after it refused to take part in the US intervention in Iraq. For Germany's former Chancellor Schröder this was a way "to temper moods in Washington" (Merz, 2007, p. 7).

Furthermore, it seems that the government's strategy has been to make the public gradually used to the reality of its mission in Afghanistan. An example for this is the fact that former Defence Minister zu Guttenberg "pushed the limits of German Afghanistan mission semantics from "stabilization mission" to "warlike conditions" to "war" "(von Bredow, 2011, p. 10). Those changes in communication of the government surely also result from an underestimation of the conflict in Afghanistan and its negative development after the unexpected Taliban resurgence in 2005/2006. Nevertheless, it becomes obvious that the German government has often played down the risks of its involvement in Afghanistan.

The above illustrated discrepancy between German elites and Post-Cold War public opinion about the role of Germany's armed forces is the reason for Germany's exaggeration of the Islamic terror threat. This finding equally explains its relatively high expenditures for development aid, which has helped Germany to justify the intervention in Afghanistan without telling the public the truth about its foreign policy ambitions. In this way, the German government was able to emphasize on two of the public's top five priorities (see section 3.1. on p. 31) for Germany's foreign and security policy to justify the Afghanistan intervention: The protection of its own citizens in combination with the enhancement of the humanitarian situation for the Afghan people, which would guarantee a certain amount of support from its electorate. In addition to that, the Afghanistan mission is not only a test for Germany alone to convince its allies of its military capacities, but also for the NATO as a whole to demonstrate its powerful role in today's complex security environment.

3.2. Hegemony and world order – A Gramscian perspective

Gramsci's theoretical framework with its concept of hegemony combined with insights coming from Global Political Economy literature about developments in the world order helps to understand why Germany gives NATO such a high priority. It reveals how Germany benefits from its contributions and how elites influence Germany's foreign policy orientation.

In the International Relation literature hegemony is used to describe the dominance of one state over the others in a world order, which was initiated by the hegemon. More generally, hegemony can be seen as the demonstration of military power that helps to protect the hegemon's political and economic power. In this regard, Kindleberger (1973, p. 305) is known for introducing the hegemonic stability theory, in which he claims the necessity of a hegemon in order to provide and maintain stability in the world order. In his theory he (Kindleberger, 1973) uses realist assumptions and focuses on power and coercion to explain the behaviour of the hegemon. This theory is not convincing and only explains one part to understand the processes of hegemony, because it neglects important features of hegemony such as consent. Therefore, Kindleberger's theory will be secondary for this research.

Opposed to that, Gramsci delivers a different idea for hegemony, which is dominating Global Political Economy literature. Apart from economic power or political-military coercion, he underlines the importance of consent (Cox, 1983, p. 164), which the hegemon needs from subordinated states to maintain stability in the initiated world order. Consequently, the created system of the hegemon needs to assure to match common interests of secondary states, where political and economic benefits can be guaranteed (see section E). This guarantee serves as the "motor force of a universal expansion" (Gramsci, 1971, p. 182) and determines success or failure of hegemony.

Many observations of Gramsci can be applied both on the international level and on the national level like for instance his emphasis on the role of ideology as well as civil society in the process of hegemony. He goes on to suggest that through a dynamic process of ideology circulation a common sense can be achieved in the civil society, which will work as a tool for dominant groups (Cox, 1983). "In this context, a class is hegemonic to the extent that it offers an integrated system of values and beliefs that support the established social order and that project a particular set of class interests as the general interest. Hegemonic power is not imposed on subordinates, but, instead, is a negotiated process [for consent]" (Egan, 2007, p. 100). The international and national promotion of neo-liberal policies through institutions, NGOs, elites and other traditional non-state actors serve as examples for this. To support his arguments and to meet requirements of a changing world order he uses an enlarged state definition, which includes not only "the executive or government but also the special apparatus of hegemony, in other words, civil society" (Gündoğan, 2008, p. 54). Gramsci's arguments are convincing and indicate a dynamic exchange between elites, who, as the dominant group, also need to provide an "intellectual and moral leadership", (Gramsci, 1971, p. 57) and the public, which implies the necessity of a common sense to maintain the hegemonic order between them.

Gramsci's theory of hegemony helps to understand Germany's foreign policy strategy. It is set up in an environment of a changing world order and a certainty of the continuity of US hegemony in the next years. Germany seems to be aware of this certainty and therefore follows a foreign policy strategy, in which it strengthens its ties with the US instead of focusing on new alliances with for example a rising power like China. The reasons for Germany's certainty about the continuity of the domination of US hegemony will be explained in the following.

The US dominancy is demonstrated in its remaining unilateral military dominance and the unquestioned acceptance of neoliberalism. Neoliberalism is, in a simplified way, defined by the promotion of policies which privilege the free market above all, as the driving ideology for the world's economic structure. The end of Great Britain's dominance of the world order during the 19th century, which was succeeded by the US in the 20th century, proved that successive hegemonies are possible. Currently, the economic development of China indicates that it will probably be able to outgrow the US as the largest economy until 2050 (IMF, 2012). China's rise in the recent years indicates the capacity of the US hegemony for two reasons. Firstly, it was able to rise faster than the US and secondly, rather than challenging the existent international institutions it continuously accepted and strengthened its position in them. An example is its entry in the WTO in 2001, which guaranteed its influence on global trade policies as well as underlined successfully its acceptance of a neo-liberal philosophy that focuses on economic growth. Consequently, Clark asserts that China "has been successful because of the order, not despite of it" (Clark, 2011, p. 25). Due to rising powers' acceptance of US established international institutions like IMF, World Bank, World Trade Organization or UN and the unilaterally dominance of the US military, it is more likely that the US will remain, at least during the first half of this century, the most influential state in the world order. Nevertheless, the economic rise of multiple large states indicates a "complex collective hegemonic order" (Clark, 2011, p. 28), without the establishment of a new international system, as a successor of the US hegemony in the future.

Furthermore, a tendency towards regionalism can be observed, which is effecting the power distribution in the world order. States increasingly join regional unions like the EU or the Association of Southeast Asian Nations (ASEAN) to be heard in the international community and to influence political-economic policies in favour of their national interests. In Germany's case this can be observed in its efforts within the EU. However, without a common foreign policy the EU as well as Germany itself with its relatively small military capacity, is not able to compete against the militaries of rising powers like China for instance. This development combined with Germany's interest to maintain its political and economic power and position in the world order explains Germany's intention to strengthen its military power under the umbrella of the US hegemony in the NATO.

Gramsci's theoretical framework can also be applied to explain Germany's decision to intervene in Afghanistan. Consent within German elites about Germany's role in shaping world politics was one of the main reasons why the German government was able to make the decision of intervening in Afghanistan. Through support from the policy planning network, the major German foreign policy Think-Tanks SWP and DGAP established the basis to contribute militarily to future international NATO missions already before 2001 (See section 3.1. on p. 30). Such an influence on major foreign policy decisions of the state become explicable when the elites together with those Think-Tanks are seen through Gramsci's perspective as a part of the dominant class and consequently also as part of the state as well as the civil society.

In this case NATO is the international organization, which provides the security umbrella for states with weaker military power like Germany under the leadership of the US. Officially, NATO's essential "purpose is to safeguard the freedom and security of its members by political and military means" (NATO, 2010, p. 6) by following its core tasks of collective defence, crises management and cooperative security. However, through acknowledging a changed security environment of e.g. asymmetrical threats, NATO's understanding of defence goes beyond the borders of its members and allows to "engage actively with other international actors before, during and after crises" (NATO, 2010, p. 19).

The reason for the US to provide this security umbrella as well as for NATOs broad defence and security definition lies in the core of US national interests. Based on Egan's (2007, p. 103) findings, the National Security Strategy of the United States of America (The White House, 2002) embodies the core ideas that also served as the basis for the decision of the US lead international intervention in Afghanistan. His findings further indicate a connection between US foreign policy and US political-economic interests. First of all, the strategy points out that the NATO alliance must act for the protection of the United States' interests (The White House, 2002, p. 25). Secondly, it emphasises that the promotion of neoliberalism is one of its core national interests and even goes further by claiming that this goes "beyond America's shores" (The White House, 2002, p. 17). Additionally, it underlines that "improving stability in emerging markets is also key to economic growth" (The White House, 2002, p. 18). Consequently, this strategy implies that the protection of neoliberalism becomes also a core task of NATO, which could even serve as a justification for a foreign military intervention. In this context Wagner (in Tal, 2010, p. 111) considers the NATO to be an actor of "neo-liberal colonialism". However, considering the amount of IOs, which are also part of a neo-liberal promotion, NATO can be considered as one more actor for the maintenance of the neo-liberal world order, which was established by the US hegemony to help the US on the on hand to receive consent through the legitimacy of an international coalition and on the other hand to share the burden for its operations.

This book argues that notably the continuation of this neo-liberal world and the benefits out of it are the reasons why Germany wants to play a major role in international organizations like NATO. As one of the world's leading export nations, whose multinational cooperation's and elites economically benefit the most from globalisation and a neo-liberal world order, it is in Germany's national interest to influence the world's political-economic decisions through a strong position in those institutions. Consequently, with the intervention in Afghanistan, Germany seems to make its contribution to the maintenance of this world order (Wagner in Tal, 2010). Apart from the maintenance of the system, such a stronger position would lead to more leverage in negotiations about consent with the US hegemon.

Finally, by ensuring a powerful role within NATO Germany serves its security interests as well as its political-economic interests on a long-term perspective. To confirm or disprove this hypothesis and to find out further motivations for Germany's intervention in Afghanistan it is necessary to analyse the economic part of Germany's intervention in Afghanistan in the following chapter.

Nonetheless, as the public polls demonstrated (see section 3.1.) the dominant class in Germany seems to be aware of the power of its people, who are unwilling to accept international military interventions under the above mentioned conditions. To maintain consent as well as stability in the state while remaining capable of acting internationally, the dominant groups need to make the public used to Germany's military contribution in future international missions. It seems that this can only happen gradually. Moreover, a narrative of success stories must be used in interventions like the one in Afghanistan to justify the war with purposes, which can be implemented in society. For this reason, this research suggests that if Germany's mission in Afghanistan can be sold as a positive contribution to security and humanity, the public's consent for the next international military intervention will be reached more easily.

4. Analysis of further political-economic interests

The analysis of political-economic interests of Germany's intervention in Afghanistan will be divided in three parts: Firstly, costs of the intervention in Afghanistan, secondly, economic benefits from the intervention, and thirdly, the geopolitical aspect of it. Indeed, an analysis of political-economic interests of the war could also discuss other areas. However, the interviews in Afghanistan combined with the literature review have shown that a cost-benefit analysis as well as geopolitical reasons are essential in the discussion about Germany's intervention in Afghanistan and simultaneously reduce the gap in the literature.

4.1. A cost-benefit analysis
First of all, it is very difficult to find reliable data about the costs of the German intervention in Afghanistan. Especially, official primary sources of the German government are rare. It seems that the German government prefers to avoid a debate about the costs of the German involvement in Afghanistan and as a consequence it does not publicise them frequently.

According to the German government, the total spending for Germany's intervention in Afghanistan had been about 5,5 billion Euros for the first ten years since 2001 (FAZ, 2011). During this period the costs had continuously increased and in 2010, Germany declared an annually spending of about one billion Euros (DIW, 2010, p. 3). During those ten years Germany also spent almost two billion Euros for development and reconstruction purposes. In the recent years, the budget for those purposes was doubled to 430 million Euros annually until 2013 (Bundesregierung, 2011, p. 70).

However, a study of the German Institute for Economic Research (DIW) estimates the costs of the German intervention in Afghanistan to be much higher than the German government has indicated. According to their research, the costs for the Afghanistan intervention in the first ten years have been around 17 billion Euros and will rise yearly about approximately two billion Euros. On the basis of this research the total costs for Germany until the troop withdrawal in the end of 2014 will be about 22 billion Euros (FAZ, 2011). The discrepancy between the calculations of the German government and the DIW can be explained through the difference in methodology. The DIW calculated the costs of the German Afghanistan intervention for the German society. Additionally, to the direct military costs of the intervention it also considered indirect costs of the intervention like for example costs that occurred in other ministries due to the Afghanistan intervention, the long-term costs due to injured or killed soldiers or the interest costs for financing the mission (DIW, 2010).

For an indication whether these costs are in proportion to the benefits of Germany's intervention in Afghanistan the benefits have to be analysed. However, the difficulty of such a cost-benefit calculation lies in the non-monetary nature of injured or deaths of both civilians and soldiers respectively benefits like for instance those resulting from an increase of international reputation.

Wagner (in Tal, 2010, pp. 111-112) argues that the history has proven that after a Western military intervention in a foreign country, a structural change in the countries economic structure, by establishing a neo-liberal free enterprise economy is immediately followed. He goes on to suggest that the same process has happened in Afghanistan after the intervention in 2001. He accuses NATO member states of pretending to intervene for reasons of security or state building in order to cover the real purpose: the implementation of a neo-liberal agenda with low taxes and simple access for foreign investors.

An analysis of the economic figures and the economic regulations of the Afghan government in the aftermath of 2001 seem to confirm Wagner's hypothesis. The import tax has dropped from 43 percent before the intervention to five percent afterwards (Wagner in Tal, 2010, p. 115), which is still valid. Compared to its neighbours or countries with similar income this is a much lower rate (Germany Trade and Invest, 2013, p. 38). Consequently, Afghanistan has been flooded with foreign goods not only from its neighbouring countries, but also from the US and Germany as one of its major import partners (Central Intelligence Agency, 2013). As a consequence national producers were eradicated from the market. The following figures illustrate this development. The import value has continuously increased from around one billion USD in 2000 to over six billion USD by 2012. Its balance of trade deficit has never been so high and peaked in the last two years with a total value of six billion USD, due to the fact that Afghanistan's exports has been maintained equal below 0,5 billion USD since 2000 (UNComtrade, 2011; Statista, 2013a). In addition to that, the former Afghan Minister of Economy stated that 99 percent of the goods in Afghanistan are imported (Handelsblatt, 2004). This implies that Afghan production facilities are almost non-existent. Moreover, it is an indication for a national economy, which was destroyed through the international intervention in Afghanistan.

An analysis of the German Afghan bilateral economic relations shows similar results. Afghanistan has been importing each year much more from Germany than it has exported to it. Regarding the last five years the average foreign trade deficit between them was about 240 million euros per year (Statistisches Bundesamt, 2013). Even if Afghanistan's import volumes have dramatically increased since the intervention, these values remain irrelevant for Germany, as a country that has one of the world leading export industries, which reached a volume of over 1000 billion euros in 2012 (Statista, 2013b).

Moreover, from the beginning of the intervention the International Monetary Fund (IMF) has supported and actively encouraged Afghanistan in its efforts to transform its economy to a neo-liberal economy by providing corresponding programmes (Wagner in Tal, 2010, p. 113). To attract private investors and assure that future policies will work in favour of this goal "the market based economy is enshrined in the Constitution, article 10, which states that: The state encourages and protects private capital investments and enterprises based on the market economy and guarantees their protection in accordance with the provisions of law" (Islamic Republic of Afghanistan, 2008, p. 73). This demonstrates that the idea of a liberal economy has been embodied in the core of the Islamic Republic of Afghanistan.

Since 2001, 90 companies from Germany have worked in this neo-liberal economic environment. They have been mainly involved in the areas of reconstruction, energy and infrastructure. Nevertheless, only 45 German enterprises are currently left in Afghanistan and are registered as a German or German-Afghan entity. Apart from the difficult security environment, the problematic for foreign investors is the high degree of corruption, bureaucratic impediments, a lack of qualified personnel and high wages compared to other developing countries (Germany Trade and Invest, 2013, p. 51). Consequently, the economic benefit for German enterprises is limited.

In the debate about economic benefits from a foreign intervention a discussion about the possibility of exploiting its resources is inevitable. Indeed, Afghanistan has a huge amount of minerals. "Afghanistan houses rich seams of copper, iron, gold, lithium and rare earth deposits worth up to $3 trillion, according to the Afghan government" (Nichol, 2011). This seems to be a beneficial business for the economies and companies of countries like the US or Germany, owing to the fact that the demand for these resources in the world is already high and increases continuously. However, the reality is that this discovery is not new. Already in times of Alexander the Great it was suspected that Afghanistan has valuable resources and minerals; and particularly, the Soviet Union put much efforts into identifying resourceful areas all over Afghanistan. The problems that the Russians faced are the same problems the international community and the Afghan government are still facing. There is almost a non-existent infrastructure, an unstable security environment and a lack of qualified personnel, which make an access to the majority of these resources impossible. Consequently, the mining industry contributes only 0,3 percent to the Afghan gross domestic product (GDP), which means that it is almost non-existent (Germany Trade and Invest, 2013, p. 21). This shows that the argument of justifying the intervention with Afghanistan's vast amount of resources has to be put into perspective.

As a consequence to the uncertainties, the Afghan government promotes its vast mineral deposits to the international community in order to assure long-term investments in this sector to build up the necessary infrastructure and develop this business opportunity for Afghanistan. Until today it has been particularly China who entered into agreements to exploit resources in Afghanistan (Mahr, 2013). The West has been cautious about major investments and long-term commitments, due to the unstable security situation. However, it seems that Afghanistan's valuable resources can be a long-term benefit from Germany's intervention, owing to the fact that the Afghan government values Germany's efforts in Afghanistan. The Afghan government stated to favour Germany also in the future in receiving contracts for the exploitation of resources (Spiegel, 2013). In addition to that, Germany enjoys also an excellent reputation within the Afghan population, which increases the possibility for beneficial future business cooperation's. In almost every interview with an Afghan in Afghanistan, Germany's positive image in Afghanistan was highlighted. Those who had experience with German aid and development institutions stated that they are convinced of the fact that in contrast to other foreigners in Afghanistan, Germany does not pursue direct economic interests with its engagement in Afghanistan (Members of the Afghan Parliament, Interview, 2013; Former Mujahideen fighter, Interview, 2013; Professors of the University of Balkh, Interviews, 2013).

Finally, the cost-benefit analysis revealed that although the international intervention in Afghanistan leads to the establishment of a neo-liberal market economy, the economic benefits for Germany out of it are on the short-term minimal compared to the enormous amount of expenses. An evaluation about future prospects is not possible yet, due to uncertainties about the development of the established neo-liberal institutions and reconstructed infrastructure, which could benefit the mining industry.

4.2. Geopolitical benefits
Already during the Russian occupation as well as during the Britain occupation of Afghanistan the geopolitical location Afghanistan's played a major role for their interventions. In the NATO intervention in Afghanistan there also seems to be an economic aspect and a political interest for foreign forces, which is related to Afghanistan's geopolitical location.

First of all, "the US is pursuing the vision of an economically integrated region in which Afghanistan will be the central stretch of a new 'Silk Road' between Central and South Asia, and the Middle East and East Asia" (Destradi et al., 2012, p. 1). An analysis of its recent foreign policy decisions show that US foreign policy interests have shifted more and more towards Asia. This can be explained through the economic rise of East and Southeast Asia over the last half-century. The regions share of world GDP doubled during this period and "increased [its] per capita income at an average growth rate almost two and a half times that in the rest of the world" (Quah, 2010, p. 1). The growing Asian economies and vast mineral as well as energy deposits in this region need to be integrated and secured in a neo-liberal world order, in which stability in this region will benefit economically and politically Western countries like the US (Destradi et al, 2012) and Germany.

Furthermore, it seems as if the region around Afghanistan will remain one of the most significant regions for conflicts in the 21st century (Baraki in Tal, 2010, p. 34). Therefore, military bases in Afghanistan enable the NATO to be present at the borders of high potential threats, which could be able to destabilize the region in the future. Being present beside China, the world's major rising power, which has tried continuously to strengthen its position and influence in the region in recent years, is a key US interest. A similar role represents Russia, which seems to consider central Asia as its area of retreat (Bergedorfer Gesprächskreis, 2007, p. 30). A further important aspect seems to be to stay close to India and Pakistan, who possess nuclear weapons (see chapter 1. on p. 18) and depend on energy resources for their growing population. Additionally, a presence next to Iran plays a role, which is accused of sponsoring extremist groups (Byman, 2005). On top of that, Iran feels threatened by the policies of the Western community and has orientated itself towards a greater cooperation with Central Asian states (Bergedorfer Gesprächskreis, 2007, p. 30). All these aspects seem to be key national interests for the US and its allies. The presence and different interests of such global players in the region around Afghanistan illustrate an essential benefit for NATO members through their presence and influence from this geopolitical location.

Conclusion

This book demonstrated that Germany has been one of the major donors and contributors for the US initiated intervention in Afghanistan. Since 2001, Germany has steadily increased its efforts in Afghanistan. For the first time after the Second World War it took military responsibility and even the lead in North Afghanistan, in a large-scale international mission within NATO. According to the German authorities, the intervention is justified by the protection from international terrorism apart from humanitarian and state building aspects in order to provide stability and prosperity in Afghanistan. Moreover, the analysis of mostly official German documents revealed that generally, the Afghanistan intervention is considered to be a success.

However, the examinations of Germany's claims reveal that Germany and its NATO allies have not achieved its main goals in Afghanistan, especially not in their aim to achieve security and stability in the region. This book doubts Germany's justification of the protection of its own security and the intention to decrease Islamic terror threat in Germany, as being the main reason for the intervention in Afghanistan. The evaluation of accessible European terrorism data revealed that the Islamic terrorism threat for Germany has not decreased since 2001. The threat development rather implies that it has risen due to worldwide spread of AQ ideology, the risen number of extremist Islamic organizations and the separate problem of home-grown terrorism. Finally, the report of the German Office of the Protection of the German Constitution directly links the intervention in Afghanistan with terrorism activities in Germany by finding out that the majority of Islamic terrorist organizations in Germany justify their activity in Germany with the German participation in the combat against Islamic terrorism and particularly with Germany's intervention in Afghanistan. However, further findings of this research put the threat into perspective. The international terrorism threat resulting from Islamic terrorism as well as Afghanistan's role in this context is overestimated. On the one hand the research demonstrated that AQ does not play a major role in Afghanistan and that the Taliban are primary fighting for national reasons. Additionally, a direct correlation between a failed Afghan state and a heightened terror threat in Germany is not academically proved. On the other hand the data from Europol about arrested religiously inspired extremist revealed that since 2001, the Islamic terrorism threat has been contained to a minimum through effective intelligence cooperation and that other national terrorism threats like left-wing or Separate terrorism pose a greater threat to European citizens than international terrorism.

This book identified a strategic calculation in favour of Germany's national interests as the reason for Germany's not scientifically tenable justification. A discrepancy between German elites, who are striving for a transformation of the German military from a defence army to an expeditionary force, which should be prepared for a stronger participation in NATO missions, and a implemented peace-loving public opinion in the aftermath of the Second World War explain the act of balance, of which Germany's government is aware. For this reason, the Afghanistan intervention enables the German government to use an official justification, which takes into account its electorate's opinion as well as Germany's international ambition to have a greater influence in political-economic decisions within US hegemony. In this regard the Afghanistan case also works as a test for Germany's military capacities in the eyes of its NATO allies.

The main theoretical framework for this book, Gramsci's assumptions about hegemony, underline the findings resulting from the security analysis. It emphasises that the maintenance of consent between the dominant groups and the public is a key for a stable society on the national level and an effective government on the international level. In this context Germany's official justifications for the intervention can be considered as evidence for the importance of constructing consent for the use of military power. It consequently proves Gramsci's theory. Furthermore, it illustrates Germany's main benefit from its foreign policy decision to intervene in Afghanistan, which is to strengthen its politic-economic influence through NATOs security umbrella under US hegemony. A short analysis of the political-economic world order suggests that the US hegemony will remain in the near future and as one of the major benefiters of neo-liberalism Germany's national interests rely on as well as continue the support for it.

Finally, the analysis of further political-economic reasons for Germany, reveal that apart from geopolitical benefits from regional stabilisation there are no other significant economic benefits, which could have encouraged Germany's intervention in Afghanistan. Although neo-liberalism was successfully promoted and implemented in the core of Afghanistan's economy, as the analysis of US hegemony suggested, Afghanistan's economy remains one of the weakest economies in the world and therefore without significant international impact.

Only on a long-term perspective through a possible exploitation of the resources and Germany's generally positive reputation within the Afghan population, economic benefits could be considered.

In conclusion, the book argues that Germany serves first of all its politic economic interests by its decision of intervening in Afghanistan. Although it also serves its basic security interests by strengthening its position in NATO and with regard to the changing security environment, it is not the security threat resulting from Islamic terrorism threat from Afghanistan, which can be used as the main reason for its intervention as the German authorities have been claiming. Moreover, this research suggests to continue monitoring whether the Afghanistan intervention with the support of Gramsci's theory about hegemony, where a discrepancy between elites and the public was the main driver for Germany's behaviour, helped to implement a consent in the civil society, which can be the basis that could drive future German foreign policy decisions.

Bibliography

Secondary Sources

Books and books' chapters

Alden, C. & Aran, A., 2012, Foreign Policy analysis: New approaches, New York: Routlegde

Atwan, A. B., 2012, After Bin Laden: Al-Qa'ida, The Next Generation, London: Saqi Books

Baraki, M., 2010, "Afghanistan – Friedhof der Imperialmächte?" ("Afghanistan – Graveyard of the imperialists?") in Tal, M. (eds.) Umganssprachlich: Krieg: Testfall Afghanistan und deutsche Politik, Köln: PapyRossa Verlag, pp.

Becker, J. M., & Wulf, H., 2011, Afghanistan: Ein Krieg in der Sackgasse (Afghanistan: A war that have come to a dead end), Berlin: LIT Verlag

Bellamy, A., 2008, Fighting Terror: Ethical Dilemmas, London: Zed Books

Burke, J., 2004, Al-Qaeda: The True story of radical Islam, London: Penguin Books

Byman, D., 2005, Deadly Connection: States that sponsor terrorism, New York: Cambridge University Press

Farmer, B. R., 2007, Understanding Radical Islam: Medieval ideology in the twenty-first century, New York: Peter Lang

Gareis, S. B. & Nolte, K., 2009, "Zur Legitimiation bewaffneter Auslandseinsätze der Bundeswehr – politische und rechtliche Dimensionen" ("For the legitimation of armed foreign interventions of the Bundeswehr – political and legal dimensions") in Jaberg, S., Biehl, H., Morhmann, G., Tomforde, M., (eds.) "Auslandseinsätze der Bundeswehr: Sozialwissenschaftliche Analysen, Diagnosen und Perspektiven", Berlin: Duncker & Humblot, pp. 27-50

Gramsci, A., 1971 in Q. & Smith, G.N., Selections from the prison notebooks of Antonio Gramsci, Lawrence & Wishart

Haid, M., 2010, "Im Einsatz für vitale Interessen – Die Bundeswehr in aller Welt" (In a mission for vital interests – The Bundeswehr in the world") in Tal, M. (eds.) Umgansprachlich: Krieg: Testfall Afghanistan und deutsche Politik, Köln: PapyRossa Verlag, pp. 90-100

Hamann, R., 2009, "Im Gleichschritt in die Sackgasse?" (With the marching in step to the dead end?") in Jaberg, S., Biehl, H., Morhmann, G., Tomforde, M., (eds.) "Auslandseinsätze der Bundeswehr: Sozialwissenschaftliche Analysen, Diagnosen und Perspektiven", Berlin: Duncker & Humblot, pp. 51-70

Hartmann, M., 2004, Elitesoziologie: Eine Einführung (Elite sociology: An Introduction), Frankfurt am Main: Campus Verlag

Jaberg, S., Biehl, H., Morhmann, G., Tomforde, M., 2009, "Auslandseinsätze der Bundeswehr: Sozialwissenschaftliche Analysen, Diagnosen und Perspektiven" (Foreign military interventions of the German armed forces: Analysis, diagnoses and perspectives from the social sciences), Berlin: Duncker & Humblot

Karlekar, H., 2012, Endgame in Afghanistan: for whom the dice rolls, New Delhi: SAGE Publications India Pvt Ltd

Kindleberger, C. P., 1973, "The world in Depression 1929-1939", London: The Penguin Press

Kühn, F. P., 2010, Sicherheit und Entwicklung in der Weltgesellschaft: Liberales Paradigma und Statebuilding in Afghanistan (Security and Development in the world: Liberal Paradigm and Statebuilding in Afghaistan), Wiesbaden: VS Verlag

Lutz, J. M. & Lutz, B., 2008, Global Terrorism, London: Routledge, 2nd edition

Morgenthau, H. J., 2006, Politics among nations: The struggle for power and peace, London: McGraw-Hill Education, 7th edition

Pape, A., 2006, Dying to win: The strategic logic of suicide terrorism, New York: Random House

Quah, D., 2010, "Post 1990s East Asian economic growth" in Ito, T. & Hahn, C. H., "The Rise of China and Structural Changes in Korea and Asia", Northampton: Edward Elgar, pp. 19-42

Rashid, A., 2009, Descent into Chaos: The U.S. and the Disaster in Pakistan, Afghanistan, and Central Asia, New York: Penguin Books

Tal, M., 2010, Umgangssprachlich: Krieg: Testfall Afghanistan und deutsche Politik (Colloquial: War: Experiment Afghanistan and German politics), Köln: PapyRossa Verlag

Wagner, J., 2010, "Deutschland und der Lackmusttest Afghanistan – Neoliberaler Kolonialismus und Zivil-Militärische Aufstandsbekämpfung" (Germany and the litmus test Afghanistan – Neoliberal Colonialism and Civil-military counterinsurgency") in Tal, M. (eds.) Umganssprachlich: Krieg: Testfall Afghanistan und deutsche Politik, Köln: PapyRossa Verlag, pp. 101-135

Woodward, B., 2010, Obama's Wars, London: Simon & Schuster

Articles and working papers

Barett, R., 2008, "Seven years after 9/11: Al-Qaida's Strenghts and Vulnerabilities", The international center for radicalisation and political science [Online]. Available at: http://icsr.info/files/ICSR%20Richard%20Barret%20Paper.pdf [Accessed 29 Mai 2013]

Belkin, P., 2010, "German foreign and security policy: Trends and transatlantic implications", Current Politics and Economics of Europe, Vol. 21, No. 2/3, pp. 211-245

Clark, I., 2011, "China and the United States: a succession of hegemonies?", International Affairs, Vol. 87, Issue 1, pp. 13-28

Coffey, L., The Heritage Foundation, 2013, "U.S. should back a robust Afghan National Security Force" [Online]. Available at http://www.heritage.org/research/reports/2013/02/afghan-national-security-force-us-should-back-a-robust-ansf [Accessed 19 August 2013]

Cox, R. W., 1983, "Gramsci, Hegemony and International Relations: An Essay in Method", Millennium Journal of International Studies, Vol. 12, No. 2, pp. 162-175

Destradi, S., Godehardt, N., Frank, A., 2012, The ISAF withdrawal from Afghanistan: Perceptions and Reactions of Regional Powers, GIGA (German Institute for Global and Area Studies), Issue 5 [Online]. Available at: http://www.giga-hamburg.de/dl/download.php?d=/content/publikationen/pdf/gf_international_1205.pdf [Accessed 28 April 2013]

Egan, D., 2007, "Globalization and the Invasion of Iraq: State power and the Enforcement of Neoliberalism", Sociological focus, Vol. 40, No. 1, pp. 98-111

FAZ, 2011, "Afghanistan-Einsatz: Zehn Jahre kosten Deutschland 17 Milliarden" ("Afghanistan-mission: Ten years cost 17 billion for Germany"), 03 October [Online]. Available at: http://www.faz.net/aktuell/politik/afghanistan-einsatz-zehn-jahre-kosten-deutschland-17-milliarden-11480569.html [Accessed 27 August 2013]

Foreign Policy, 2009, "The failed state index", 22 June [Online]. Available at: http://www.foreignpolicy.com/articles/2009/06/22/the_2009_failed_states_index [Accessed 11 September 2013]

Fromkin, D. 1975, "The Strategy of Terrorism", Foreign Affairs, Vol. 53, No. 4, pp. 683-698

Germany Trade and Invest, 2013, "Wirtschaftsleitfaden – Afghanistan: Perspektiven der Zusammenarbeit" (manual for the economy – Afghanistan: Perspectives and cooperation) [Online]. Available at: http://www.giz.de/de/downloads/giz2013-de-wirtschaftsleitfaden-afghanistan.pdf [Accessed 29 April 2013]

Gündoğan, E., 2008, „Conceptions of Hegemony in Antonio Gramsci's Southern Question and the Prison Notebooks", Journal of Marxism and Interdisciplinary Inquiry, Vol. 2, No. 1, pp. 45-60

Hacke, C., 2012, "Deutsche Außen und Sicherheitspolitik in Turbulenzen: Zivilmacht ohne Zivilcourage?" ("German foreign and security policy in turbulence: civil power without courage?" [Online]. Available at: http://www.kas.de/wf/doc/kas_29999-544-1-30.pdf?120209165246 [Accessed 29 April 2013]

Handelsblatt, 2004, "Erste Milliardenprojekte für Afghanistan" ("First multi billion projects for Afghanistan"), 31 March [Online]. Available at: http://www.handelsblatt.com/politik/international/deutsche-firmen-unter-investoren-bisher-kaum-vertreten-erste-milliardenprojekte-fuer-afghanistan/2317586.html [Accessed 29 April 2013]

Hassan, O. & Hammond, A., 2011, "The rise and fall of American's freedom agenda in Afghanistan: Counter-terrorism, nation-building and democracy", The International Journal of Human Rights, Vol. 15, No. 4, pp. 532-551

Hehir, A., 2007, "The Myth of the Failed State and the War on Terror: A Challenge to the Conventional Wisdom", Journal of Intervention and Statebuilding, Vol. 1, No. 3, pp. 307-332

Hein, P., 2011, "In the Shadow of Pacifism: Foreign Policy Choices of Germany and Japan in Afghanistan", East Asia, Vol. 28, No. 2, pp. 135-155

Herwartz, C., 2012, "Afghanistan Einsatz läuft aus: Kapitualtion vor der Realität" ("Afghanistan mission is ending: Capitulation from the reality"), n-tv, 29 November [Online]. Available at: http://www.n-tv.de/politik/Kapitulation-vor-der-Realitaet-article9630721.html [Accessed 07 August 2013]

Keller, P., 2009, Argumente für Afghanistan: Ein Leitfaden für die Debatte (Arguments for Afghanistan: A manual for the debate), Konrad Adenauer Stiftung Analysen & Argumente, Vol. 66, [Online]. Available at: http://www.kas.de/wf/de/71.4924/?623_1_ft_string=afghanistan+interessen&submit_search= Suche&form_id=623_29&change_lang=&623_start_line=1&623_lines_per_page=10 [Accessed 07 May 2013]

Laqueur, W., 1996, "Postmodern Terrorism", Foreign Affairs, Vol. 75, No. 5, pp. 24-36

Mahr, K., 2013, "Treasure Land: Afghanistan's mountains are rich in untapped minerals that could prove to be a blessing- and a curse", TIME, vol. 182, No. 11, pp. 26-33

Meiers, F.J., 2010, "Von der Scheckbuchdiplomatie zur Verteidigung am Hindukusch. Die Rolle der Bundeswehr bei multinationalen Auslandseinsätzen 1990-2009" ("From a chequebook diplomacy towards a defence at the Hindukusch. The role of the Bundeswehr within multinational foreign interventions from 1990-2009"), Zeitschrift für Außen- und Sicherheitspolitik, Vol. 3, No. 2, pp. 201-222

Merz, S., 2007, "Still on the Way to Afghanistan? Germany and its forces in the Hindu Kush", Stockholm International Peace Research Institute (SIPRI) [Online]. Available at: http://www.sipri.org/research/conflict/publications/merz [Accessed 18 April 2013]

Meyer, B., 2007, "Von der Entgrenzung nationaler deutscher Interessen: Die politische Legitimation weltweiter Militäreinsätze" ("From the boundary of German national interests: The political legitimation of worldwide military interventions"), Hessische Stiftung Friedens und Konfliktforschung, Vol. 10 [Online]. Available at: http://www.hsfk.de/fileadmin/downloads/report1007.pdf [Accessed 05 September 2013]

Miko, F. T. & Froehlich, C., 2004, "Germany's role in fighting terrorism: Implications for U.S. Policy, Congressional Research Service" [Online]. Available at: http://www.dtic.mil/dtic/tr/fulltext/u2/a444776.pdf [Accessed 08 May 2013]

Nichol, E., theguardian, 2011, "Afghanistan's vast mineral deposits could lift it out of poverty", 12 October [Online]. Available at: http://www.theguardian.com/global-development/poverty-matters/2011/oct/12/afghanistan-transparency-vast-mineral-deposits [Accessed 08 May 2013]

Noetzel, T. & Schreer, B., 2008, "All the way?: The evolution of German Military Power", International Affairs, Vol. 84, No. 2, pp. 211-221

Piazza, J. A., 2008, "Incubators of Terror: Do Failed and Failing States Promote Transnational Terrorism?", International Studies Quarterly, Issue 52, pp. 469-488

Risse, T., 2004, "Kontinuität durch Wandel: Eine "neue" deutsche Außenpolitik?" ("Continuity through change: A "new" German foreign policy?"), Aus Politik und Zeitgeschichte, Vol. B11, pp. 24-31

Rollins, J., 2011, "Al Qaeda and its affiliates: Historical Perspective, Global Presence, and Implications for U.S. Policy", [Online]. Available at: http://www.fas.org/sgp/crs/terror/R41070.pdf [Accessed 12 August 2013]

Simons, A. & Tucker, D., 2007, "The misleading Problem of Failed States: a 'socio-geography' of terrorism in the post-9/11 era", Third World Quaterly, Vol. 28, No. 2, pp. 387-401

SPIEGEL, P., 2009, "Bundeswehr-Mission: Merkel wirbt für Fortsetzung von Afghanistan-Einsatz" ("Bundeswehr-mission: Merkel promotes the continuation of the Afghanistan mission"), 18 September [Online]. Available at: http://www.spiegel.de/politik/ausland/bundeswehr-mission-merkel-wirbt-fuer-fortsetzung-von-afghanistan-einsatz-a-649796.html [Accessed 08 August 2013]

SPIEGEL, 2013, "Rohstoff Offensive: Deutsche Firmen sollen bei Bergbau in Afghanistan helfen" ("Attack on raw materials: German companies shall aid the mining industry in Afghanistan"), 05 July [Online]. Available at: http://www.spiegel.de/wirtschaft/unternehmen/deutsche-firmen-sollen-bei-bergbau-in-afghanistan-helfen-a-909622.html [Accessed 29 August 2013]

Starvidris, J., "The 15.000 Troop option: Plotting the course for post-2014 Afghanistan"., Foreign Policy, 13 August, [Online]. Available at: http://www.foreignpolicy.com/articles/2013/08/13/the_15000_troop_option_afghanistan?page=0,0 [Accessed 15 August 2013]

Steinberg. G., 2009, "Terror-Anschläge: Deutschland stärker gefährdet als USA", (Terro-attacks: Germany is in greater risk than the USA), Die Presse, 31 January [Online]. Available at: http://diepresse.com/home/politik/aussenpolitik/448748/TerrorAnschlaege_Deutschland-staerker-gefaehrdet-als-USA [Accessed 05 Mai 2013]

Sydow, C., 2013, "Qaida-Hochburg Yemen: Das neue Herz des Terrors" ("Qaida-Stronghold Yemen: The new heart of terrorism"), SPIEGEL, 07 August [Online]. Available at: http://www.spiegel.de/politik/ausland/jemen-ist-das-neue-afghanistan-als-hochburg-von-al-qaida-a-915374.html [Accessed 15 August 2013]

Van Linschoten, A. S. & Kuehn, F., 2011, "Separating the Taliban from al-Qaeda: The Core of Success in Afghanistan", Center of International Cooperation [Online]. Available at: http://cic.es.its.nyu.edu/sites/default/files/gregg_sep_tal_alqaeda.pdf [Accessed 15 August 2013]

Von Bredow, W., 2011, "Germany in Afghanistan: The Pitfalls of Peace Building in National and International Perspective", Res Militaris, Vol. 2, No. 1

Primary Sources

Official documents and reports

Bergedorfer Gesprächskreis, 2007, 137. Bergedorfer Gesprächskreis: Europäische Politik in Zentralasien (137. Bergedorfer Gesprächskreis: Eurpean Policy in Central Asia), [Online]. Available http://www.koerber-stiftung.de/fileadmin/user_upload/internationale_politik/bergedorder_gespraechskreis/pdf/2007/bnd_137_de.pdf [Accessed 09 September 2013]

Bundesamt für Verfassungsschutz, 2001-2011, Verfassungsschutzbericht (Report from the office for the Protection of the German Constitution), [Online]. Available http://www.verfassungsschutz.de/de/oeffentlichkeitsarbeit/publikationen/verfassungsschutzberichte [Accessed 16 August 2013]

Bundesregierung, 2011, Fortschrittsbericht Afghanistan: Zur Unterrichtung des Deutschen Bundestags (Progress report: For providing information to the German Bundestag), December [Online]. Available at: https://www.auswaertiges-amt.de/cae/servlet/contentblob/605112/publicationFile/163004/Afghanistan_Fortschritt.pdf [Accessed 10 August 2013]

Bundesregierung, 2013a, Das deutsche Engagement in Afghanistan (The German engagement in Afghanistan), 01 March [Online]. Available at: http://www.bundesregierung.de/Content/DE/HTML/Breg/Anlagen/infografik-afghanistan-textversion-neu.pdf;jsessionid=79B767977DD6841B65A5BF3079FECB72.s3t2?__blob=publicationFile&v=6 [Accessed 06 August 2013]

Bundesregierung, 2013b, Fortschrittsbericht Afghanistan: Zur Unterrichtung des Deutschen Bundestags (Progress report: For providing information to the German Bundestag), 18 Juni [Online]. Available at: http://www.auswaertiges-amt.de/cae/servlet/contentblob/649670/publicationFile/181971/130624_Zwischenbericht_Juni_2013_Download.pdf [Accessed 10 August 2013]

Bundesministerium der Justiz, 2013, Grundgesetz (German Constitution), [Online]. Available at: http://www.gesetze-im-internet.de/gg/art_87a.html [Accessed 21 August 2013]

Bundesministerium der Verteidigung, 1992, Verteidigungspolitischen Richtlinien vom 26. November 1992 (Guidelines from the Ministry of Defence from the 26. of November 1992) 26 November [Online]. Available at: http://www.asfrab.de/fileadmin/user_upload/media/pdf/VPR1992.pdf [Accessed 21 August 2013]

Bundesministerium der Verteidigung, 2006, Weißbuch 2006: Zur Sicherung Deutschlands und zur Zukunft der Bundeswehr (Whitebook 2006: For the security of Germany and to the future of the Bundeswehr) 25 October [Online]. Available at: http://www.bmvg.de/portal/a/bmvg/!ut/p/c4/Dca7DYAwDAXAWVgg7unYAuicYCVP-Qrnsz7omqObfoUnPHfUwolOuhx2u4zN0xuFC_IGQddWEzqi4eLF1i7mqXFkKf-WQNUOF6jFY_sAY_7e5g!!/ [Accessed 21 August 2013]

Bundesministerium der Verteidigung, 2013, ISAF – Im Einsatz für die Stabilisierung Afghanistans (ISAF – In mission for the stability of Afghanistan), [Online]. Available at: http://www.bmvg.de/portal/a/bmvg/!ut/p/c4/JYlBDoMwDATf0g_E9974Be0lcmCTWFCDYg MSrydSNYeRZuhLHeVTCrtsyiuN9Jnkna6QfmcJJlNFqxC3fVvFZQkQNfY75gMtztCYm6D 7P-A3em0xHTrDLtQWOJfKKuastC_D6wEWFKYD/ [Accessed 06 August 2013]

DIW, 2010, Eine erste Schätzung der wirtschaftlichen Kosten der deutschen Beteiligung am Krieg in Afghanistan (A first estimation of the economical costs of the German participation in the War in Afghanistan), Wochenbericht No. 21 [Online]. Available at: http://www.diw.de/documents/publikationen/73/diw_01.c.356890.de/10-21-1.pdf [Accessed 29 April 2013]

Europol, 2013, TE-SAT 2013: EU Terrorism situation and trend report [Online]. Available at: https://www.europol.europa.eu/sites/default/files/publications/europol_te-sat2013_lr_0.pdf [Accessed 15 April 2013]

Europol, 2007-2013, TE-SAT: EU Terrorism situation and trend report [Online]. Available at: https://www.europol.europa.eu/latest_publications/37 [Accessed 15 April 2013]

Islamic Republic of Afghanistan, 2008, Afghanistan National Development Strategy, [Online]. http://www.embassyofafghanistan.org/sites/default/files/publications/Afghanistan_National_ Development_Strategy_eng.pdf [Accessed 30 August 2013]

NATO, 2010, Strategic Concept, [Online]. Available at: http://www.nato.int/nato_static/assets/pdf/pdf_publications/20120214_strategic-concept-2010-eng.pdf [Accessed 26 August 2013]

Statistisches Bundesamt, 2013, Statistisches Jahrbuch, [Online]. Available at: https://www.destatis.de/DE/Publikationen/StatistischesJahrbuch/StatistischesJahrbuch2012.pd f?__blob=publicationFile [Accessed 28 August 2013]

The White House, 2002, The National Security Strategy of the United States of America, [Online]. Available at: http://www.state.gov/documents/organization/63562.pdf [Accessed 14 September 2013], pp. 1-31

UNComtrade, 2011, Afghanistan, [Online]. Available at: http://www.google.de/url?sa=t&rct=j&q=&esrc=s&source=web&cd=3&ved=0CEIQFjAC&u rl=http%3A%2F%2Fcomtrade.un.org%2Fpb%2FFileFetch.aspx%3FdocID%3D4 319%26type%3Dcountry%2520pages&ei=lXQgUpOfJqGu4QS9r4GgCw&usg=AFQjCNHe Ml0NvurKnNkmJOj1a12dUTIUwA&bvm=bv.51495398,d.bGE [Accessed 19 August 2013]

United Nations Assistant Mission in Afghanistan, 2013, Afghanistan: Annual Report 2012, Protections of civilians in armed conflict, [Online]. Available at: http://unama.unmissions.org/LinkClick.aspx?fileticket=K0B5RL2XYcU%3D&tabid=12254&language=en-US [Accessed 19 August 2013]

Personal interviews

Former high representative of the National Directorate of Security, Kabul (Afghanistan), personal interview, 07 July 2013

Former Mujahideen fighter, Mazar-I-Sharif (Afghanistan), personal interview, 01 July 2013

Former member of the Ministry of Commerce and Industries, Mazar-I-Sharif (Afghanistan), personal interview, 28 June 2013

High representative of the Ministry of Labor, Social Affairs, Martyrs & Disabled, Kabul (Afghanistan), personal interview, 06 July 2013

High representative governing northern Afghanistan, Mazar-I-Sharif (Afghanistan), personal interview, 04 July 2013

High representative of the National Directorate of Security, Kabul (Afghanistan), personal interview, 08 July 2013

International Law professor at the Balkh University, Mazar-I-Sharif (Afghanistan), personal interview, 27 June 2013

Members of the Afghan Parliament, Kabul (Afghanistan), personal interview with two members of the Afghan Parliament, 08 July 2013

Political Science professor at the Balkh University, Mazar-I-Sharif (Afghanistan), personal interview, 27 June 2013

Senior member of the German Embassy Kabul, Kabul (Afghanistan), personal interview, 08 July 2013

More information about the personal interviews can be found in the "Methodology and case study section" of the Introduction

Published talks

Obama, B., 2009, Remarks by the President in address to the Nation on the Way Forward in Afghanistan and Pakistan, Talk given at the United States Military Academy at West Point, West Point, 01 December [Online]. Available at: http://www.whitehouse.gov/the-press-office/remarks-president-address-nation-way-forward-afghanistan-and-pakistan [Accessed 20 July 2013]

Schröder, G., 2001, Rede im Deutschen Bundestag (Speech in the German Bundestag), Berlin, 12. September [Online]. Available at: http://dip21.bundestag.de/dip21/btp/14/14186.pdf [Accessed 05 Mai 2013]

Shea, J., 2009, "International terrorism: is it still a strategic threat?, Lecture at the NATO, 22 December [Online]. Available at: http://www.nato.int/cps/en/natolive/opinions_84764.htm [Accessed 19 September 2013]

Struck, P., 2002 a, Pressekonferenz mit Minister Struck zur Weiterentwicklung der Bundeswehr (Press conference with minister Struck about the further development of the Bundeswehr), Talk given at the ministry of defence, Berlin, 05 December [Online]. Available at:
http://www.bmvg.de/portal/a/bmvg/!ut/p/c4/NY3BCsIwEET_KGkOFetNUUEPetR6KWmyp ItNUjabevHjTYXOwBzmDYx8yeKgZ3SaMQY9yqdsDe76j-
j97lTHgImBMHvhIJkBzcDQ_dkMxIAWXQ4urcMuAXKnmroWliYoTWLK5i0fy5MFYWI AXpIhMJZ0pDmSmCLxuJBMVIhAK9tKHQ-Vqlap72bbXk9NqS63811O3u9_-L2Ycw!!/
[Accessed 06 August 2013]

Struck, P., 2002 b, Rede im Deutschen Bundestag zur Verlängerung des ISAF-Mandats (Speech in the German Bundestag (Lower House of Parliament) about the extension of the ISAF mandate), Talk given at the German Bundestag, Berlin, 20 December [Online]. Available at:
http://www.bmvg.de/portal/a/bmvg/!ut/p/c4/NY0xC4MwFIT_UWKKFuxm6dLBqUO1i8TkE R81ibw87dIf31jwDm647-
DkS2YHvaHTjDHoWXayN3gZP2L0mxMeAyYGwtULB8lMaCaG4c82IAa06Nbg0jEcEiAP qq4qYWmB3CSm1bzlc3-yIEwMwHsyBMacjjRHEksknneyEmUi0Mq-
ULdroYpD6nsuu_rU1FXZtveHXLxvfg5POEU!/ [Accessed 06 August 2013]

Websites

Bundesministerium des Inneren, Häufig gestellte Fragen zum Thema: Islamischer Terrorismus (Frequently asked questions to the topic: Islamic terrorism) [Online]. Available at:
http://www.bmi.bund.de/SharedDocs/FAQs/DE/Themen/Sicherheit/Islamismus/01.html [Accessed 16 August 2013]

Bundeswehr, ISAF – Einsatz in Afghanistan (ISAF – Mission in Afghanistan), [Online]. Available at:
http://www.bundeswehr.de/portal/a/bwde/!ut/p/c4/04_SB8K8xLLM9MSSzPy8xBz9CP3I5Ey rpHK9pPKUVL3UzLzixNSSqlS93MziYqCK1Dy9zOLENP2CbEdFAAm5vGk!/ [Accessed 06 August 2013]

Central Intelligence Agency, The World Factbook, [Online]. Available at:
https://www.cia.gov/library/publications/the-world-factbook/geos/af.html [Accessed 11 September 2013]

Icasualties, Coalition Military Fatalities by year, [Online]. Available at:
http://icasualties.org/OEF/Index.aspx [Accessed 19 August 2013]

IMF, 2012, International Monetary Fund, World Economic and Financial Surveys, World Ecnomic Outlook Database [Online]. Available at:
http://www.imf.org/external/pubs/ft/weo/2012/02/weodata/index.aspx [Accessed 11 April 2013]

Statista, Handelsbilanz von Afghanistan 2012 (Trade balance of Afghanistan 2012) [Online]. Available at: http://de.statista.com/statistik/daten/studie/256588/umfrage/handelsbilanz-von-afghanistan/ [Accessed 30 August 2013a]

Statista, Wert der Deutschen Exporte bis 2012 (Value of the German exports until 2012) [Online]. Available at: http://de.statista.com/statistik/daten/studie/165463/umfrage/deutsche-exporte-wert-jahreszahlen/ [Accessed 30 August 2013b]